Journal of Joseph V[...] of Salem

November, 1813—April, 1815

With other papers relating to his experience in Dartmoor Prison.

MICHIGAN SOCIETY
OF
COLONIAL WARS

1922

Three hundred copies printed, of which this is No. 158

PREPARED FOR PUBLICATION

BY THE

BURTON HISTORICAL COLLECTION

DETROIT PUBLIC LIBRARY

all hands then turned too our pumps and we stopt the
Leak in a few Minuets our enemie was by this in
a Croud of sail Endeavouring to get clear of us
but our Leak being stopt and we all taking a Stiff
Dram we went to our sweeps and swept towards
a Portuguese Brig who stood a Silent Spectator to our
Unpleasant play we Boarded her and took out Several
Boxes of Orange's and learnt by her that the Enemy
was a Brig of war Mounting fourteen Guns and Ninty
Men we took in our Boat and stowed her and then
Opening the boxes we ate up all the Oranges and
then went to our sweeps again like hardy tars
and with a light breeze of wind we had the
pleasure of being along of him by Dark when
we began our play again and Continued it until ten

From the entry for May 1, 1814.

Introduction

TO ONE whose ancestry goes back to those who went "down to the sea in ships," there is always a lure and a fascination about the sea and the old seaport towns, especially if the town be in old New England. Consequently those were interesting days spent last summer in the Essex Institute and Peabody Museum, Salem, searching through old ships' logs, time-worn newspapers, contemporaneous journals, books of shipping news and nautical history, to find material to supplement and form a background for this diary of a seafaring relative, one Joseph Valpey. The manuscript was given several years ago to the writer's father, Lewis Nelson Valpey, by his aunt, Mrs. Mehitable Valpey Atwill, of Arlington, Massachusetts, and after his death was purchased by Mr. C. M. Burton. L. N. Valpey's father, Joseph Hodges Valpey, once of Lynn, but for the last thirty years of his life a resident of Detroit, Michigan, was a namesake and nephew of the diarist.

In the voluminous diary of William Bentley, pastor of the East Church, Salem, are to be found references to the Valpey family, with frequent allusions to their seemingly constant anxiety for fathers and sons at sea, for whom prayer was freqeuently requested of the church.

On June 24, 1792, there was an entry in the register of the East Church of the baptism of Joseph Valpey, Jr., aged three days, son of Joseph and Mehitable Murray Valpey. A note in the diary of the same Pastor Bentley, who apparently recorded the minutest details in the lives of his parishioners, mentions the fact that the father was at sea at the time of this child's birth. Slight wonder that he, too, followed the seas.

Joseph Valpey, Sr., is mentioned by Bowdoin B. Crowninshield in his article, *An account of the private armed ship "Amer-*

ica" of Salem, published in Volume 37 of the Historical Collections of the Essex Institute. The entry reads as follows:

" 'Nov. 24 at 7:30 A. M. saw a sail bearing S. W. by S. steering to the E. S. E. Made all necessary sail in chase.

'At 9 A. M. brought her to and boarded her: she proved to be the British ship Hope from St. Thomas for Glasgow, 45 days out, Gilbert Clemons master: Full Cargo: Sugar and Rum. He informed us that he had left the fleet 4 days before, consisting of thirty-two sail of merchantmen under the convoy of the Ring Dove, Sloop of war.' This was the sort of dove-cote in which such a hawk as the America produced the wildest terror. 'Put on board Joseph Valpey, prize master and twelve men: took several small articles and the prisoners from her and ordered her to America. Lat. 46° 35'.'

The 'small articles' referred to usually included quadrant, spyglass, and samples of cargo and sometimes small arms and specie, but never the personal property of the prisoners."

Acknowledgment is gratefully made to Miss Jennie Valpey and Mr. Fred Valpey of Lynn and Mrs. Annie Manwell of Arlington, Massachusetts, for information regarding family history and the loan of letters written by Joseph Valpey, Jr., and other historical data. Two of the letters are printed here; the others were written home during his earlier voyages to Smyrna, Malta, and other eastern Mediterranean ports. They are all addressed to his parents and reveal a touching family affection and the longings of a homesick boy for home and loved ones. In one letter reference is made to the ravages of Napoleon Bonaparte's ships on the Mediterranean, and to the hazards of the deep in those troublous times.

Joseph Valpey, Sr., was part owner of the privateer schooner "Herald" of New York, commanded by Capt. John Miller, which may have been one reason that his son, Joseph, shipped on that particular vessel after several other voyages on various merchant ships. It appears from one of the old letters which are herewith printed, that he reached his decision to board a privateer only after considerable hesitation and mental struggle, but having once made up his mind, he was eager to be off.

The story of his sea experiences and of his life as a British prisoner of war are so vividly told by him in the following pages, that more need not be said by way of preface. The diary, however, leaves the reader wondering as to what came next. Old family records tell us that he died at sea, on his way home, on March 24, 1816, and was buried in Havana, Cuba. His diary came home to his sorrowing family in his sea chest with his other belongings. With all that it tells of his adventures and trying experiences on land and sea—experiences shared by many another homesick lad of those days—it is no wonder that the worn little volume was treasured by his family and handed down for coming generations to read.

Detroit, April, 1922. E. G. V.

The Travels and Sufferings of Joseph Valpey Jun͏ͬ, of Salem

IT was on November the 2 1813 i ship'd on Board of the Letter of Marque Schooner Monkey of Boston, John H Glov[er] Master Bound to Charleston S C and from thence . . . * We lay at Boston until the twenty fifth waiting [for] Freight and on the twenty sixth we dropped down to th[e] Castle and took in our Long Boat and got all Ready for Sea on the twenty seventh we weighed our anchor and proce[eded] out to sea with a pleasant Breeze from W N W but it ch[anged? We] put back for Marblehead where we Arived about four [in] the Afternoon it being on fryday we cleared up the d[eck. T]hought on ho[me] Saturday, it being very Cold [and the Win]d being to [the eas]tward and know[ing] that [we couldn't proceed] to sea we asked permission from our Captain [to go home] to which he refused to do replying that up [on a] favourable wind we should start in the afternoon. [Having received] his answer we made ourselves contented that night and [the] next morning it being pleasant we made ourselves [contente]d until after dinner when John Williams S Abbot [Wi]llis and myself took our Bags and Beding up on [deck] with the intention to leave the Monkey our Captain [per]ceiving this he enquiring what we was going to do, we Answered him that we was going to leave the schooner if [we c]ould not have the Liberty to visit home then he gave [con]sent

---

*The *Journal* of Joseph Valpey, Jr., came to the Burton Historical Collection unbound, a compact little book, which might easily have been slipped into the pocket of a greatcoat. Several of its leaves were quite badly torn, as will be seen from the frequent breaks in the narrative on this and following pages. The substance of the *Journal* was printed in the Boston Herald of March 9, 1902. This article has been mounted by a member of the family, in a booklet, on the first page of which, the same loving hand has copied the first page of the *Journal,* evidently before that page was so badly torn. By this means, several missing words have been supplied. To avoid the frequent repetition of the explanatory word "torn," omissions have been indicated by dots.

[2]

that all that did belong to salem might go [but at t]he same time he wished that we would return early [next mor]ning to which we Con[sented] and then there being eight that did belong to salem we sat out for Salem it being about three p. m. where we Arived Just before Dark, and early the next morning we returned back and cleared ship for getting under way but the wind hauling Round to the eastward we let all stand on Tuesday Morning there being a pleasant Breeze from the Westward we weighed our Anchor and proceeded for Cape Ann as that being a harbour that we could loo[k] into the bay we came to anchor about noon where We lay until fryday when about four in the morning the Breeze springing up from the N W our Captain Went on shore upon a large hill that stood Near the Sea side and seeing that the bay was clear of cruisers he returned on Board and gave the Joyful News for getting under way we weighed our Anchor and proceeded out with a pleasant Breeze at eight we sat the Squarsail and top gallant sail at half past one P M the Man at Masthead discovered a sail standing in the bay but we soon perceived her to be a British all hands was quickly called for to take in the Squarsail and top gallant sail as the wind by this time had hauled round to the N E and began for to snow and blowing very heavy and in taking in the Squarsail it split from head to clue but we soon had our little ship on the wind to the southward & eastward And our enemy in clost persuit of us with all Canvas crowded at four in the afternoon the Breeze Freshning we took one reef in the Mainsail at half past five we Carryed away our Main Boom which was the occasion of Breaking our second Mates Leg and Wounded J Williams [an]d myself slightly but not minding our Slighty wounds we turned too and hauled in the Mainsail which was a towing alongside at six our fore gaft went which obliedged Us for to lower down the fore sail and we had but Just time enough for to stow away the foresail when the fore yard went into three peices which caused us for to furl the topsail and our Jibbs being all the sail that we could set put our helm alea thinki[ng] that we could not Escape our enemy but at half past Seven as the Lord would have it our enemy passed us Within gun shot with all sail set but it snowing so thick and it being very dark they did not percei[ve] Us, the next Morning it being our Watch on deck after taking a stiff dram we proceeded for to clear away the fore yard which was left hanging all Night but it being very cold and snowing it was som[e] time before we cleared the wreck at eight the next Morning having got all

snug and the decks cleared up we Turned too for to fish the
Main boom and fore gaft Which we compleated in three days
and then taking Our squarsail boom for a fore yard we soon had
our Little ship in ample order again but not for Carrying sail
Nothing worth our Notice occurd Until the twenty-fourth Ins^t
when at day light the Man at Mast head discovered a sail on
our Lea Bow but could not make her out at Nine she comi[n]g
Up with us we perceived her to be an armed schooner Standing
for us we then tacked ship and stood from her and the Breeze
freshning and she coming up with Us very fast when at ½ past
two in the afternoon we had the pleasure for to see his fore gaft
carryed away which caused him for to give up the Chase & Re-
lieve us from the hands of our enemy as we Supposed him to be,
Nothing More until the twenty Ninth when to our great Joy we
discovered Land it being about three in the afternoon we stood
in for the Light house until six then seing no pilot Coming off
we shortned sail and stood off and on Until daylight the next
Morning when we Made All the sail that our crazy ship would
carry & stood in for the Buoy's—it being now on the Thirtyeth
at ten in the Morning we received A pilot on board and at one in
the afternoon we came to anchor in the stream and at six we
hauled in along side of the wharf and safe Moord our little
barque after a long and tegeous passag[e] The next Morning we
began for to discharge our Cargo which consisted of Fruit potatoes hay hardware Glass &c with which we Cleared our little
Barque of the next day when the Embargo was put on all Ships
and vessels then laying within the ports of the United States
which caused us for to lay idle until we could receive orders
from home which was not until the fifteenth of February 1814
When our captain received orders from home to dismantle our
Schooner and discharge all Hands in striping our Masts we discovered that both of them was Sprung very badly on Monday
the seventeenth at Nine in the Morning we all went up to the agents
store and was paid off at the rate of twenty dollars per Month
and then we repaird on Board and took Breakfast and at eleaven
Myself with six of My Shipmates went up to the Rendervous
and entered on Board of the privateer schooner Herald of New
York John Miller Commander Bound on a cruise of four Months*
and then i went down again and saw John Williams—S Abbot
and B Willis Embark on Board of a Small packet for Wilminton
N C and From thence to proceed home—since i have been Im-

---

*See letter, page 29.

form[e]d that on there arival at wilmington they purchased an old horse and Cart and arived safe at New York when there Horse died and then they Sold there cart and traveld for salem which they Compleated in fifty days on the Nineteenth Not wishing for to stay on shore any longer and eager to Get to sea again and try My luck i went on Board And Joined the ship's crew on sunday Morning it being on the twenty first at ten in the forenoon we weighed our Anchor and firing a salute of seventeen guns and then proceeded down for Rebellion roads and there wait for a Wind where we lay until the twenty sixth in the Morning when our Captain and pilot came on Board and Gave orders for getting under way all Hands being amediately Called and with Joy and gladness in every heart we was soon Under way with the saucy Jack Privateer in company at three in the afternoon it came up squally we carryed away our fore Yard in the slings which caused us to put Back for Charleston at sundown it clearing off the Man at Mast head discovered a sail standing for the Land supposing her for to be .the Dotterel a British Brig of War then on that station all hands was called to Quarters where We Stayed until daylight the next Morning as the night and rainy and we did not wish to be surpris[e]d by our Enemy We lay clost in under the Bar all night and the next Morning we began for to fire signal guns of distress for a Pilot at eleven A M we dispatched our second Lieutenant with six Men for to go on Board of the United States Schooner Nonsuch for a pilot but she returned and could not procure one we clost Reeft our Lower sails and kept in clost to the bar with a Continual firing of signal guns until dark at seven [in the] Morning we received a pilot on Board which con [ducted us] into Rebellion roads our Captain went directly up . . . and had a nother Yard Made which was finish[ed that] Day and towed along side then we swayed it . . . Rig'd it and sent it aloft and in a few . . . all ready for sea again on the first day of [March] being a pleasant Breeze from the westward we weighed our anchor and proceeded to sea having on Board one Hundred and twenty Brisk young Men for to try our Luck and fortune on Board of the Herald of Eleven Carriage gun's at four in the afternoon the Man at Masthead discovered a sail all hands was called to Make sail in chase we soon came up with her she proved for to be a Spanish Brig from Havannah [bound] to Philidelphia the next day we Boarded an . . . schooner bound to Boston ——— Nothing More . . . [until] the thirtyeth of March when the Man at [mast head] Discovered land it proved to be the . . . [Ma]deira we ran down a long shore under easy . . . next Morning we discovered a sail in shore . . . chase and soon came up with her she proved for to be an Portuguese brig from Madeira Bound to London after taking out two Casks of wine one Cable and some Letters and Bills of Exchange to the amount of three thousand dollars and getting the Imformation of an English Letter of Marque in Madeira Bound to London the first wind we permited them to proceed here we cruised for several day's but seeing no Letter of Marque we bore up for Cadis Nothing Material Occurd until the eighteenth of April when the Man at Mast head discovered a sail all hands was called for to Make sail in chase we soon came up with her she proved for to be the English Merchant Brig Signet with a cargo of wine and barley after taking our prisoners out we put a prize master and Crew on Board and ordered her for the United States on the twentyeth sail O again was the Cry of the Man at the Mast head all hands was called for to Make sail in chase after coming up with her she proved to be the English Merchant Brig Harriot in Ballast after taking out the Prisoners, Sails and provisions &c we burnt her there it appears that the Lord does favour us we steering away to the Eastward under easy sail until the twenty third we discovered a Brig Endeavoring to shun us if possible but we soon in a Cloud of Sail overhauled her She proved for to be the English Merchant Brig Place in Ballast after taking out the Prisoners, sails provisions and four twelve Pound Cannonades we burnt her that Evening We Boarded an Portuguese brig and put all of our Prisoners on Board and ordered her to Lisbon by the prisoners request early in the Morning on the twenty Eighth the Man at Mast head discovered a sail on Boarding her we found her to be the same Brig that we ordered for the United States on the Eighteenth Ins. the prize master in hope's of Making his fortune put back for Cadis but he was received on Board of the Privateer again and put in Confinement and one of our foremast Men was put on Board and ordered for the States then we bore up to the Northward and eastward and on the first day of May at daylight we discovered a large Ship and a brig it being Moderate all Hands was amediately Called for to out sweep's we

Swept to windward of them and then Observing that they
wished for to keep clear from us we in Sweeps and then went
to breakfast after Breakfast all Hands was called to Quarters
and sweeps again and hoisting our Coleurs and then all Hands
with cheerful hearts turned too and by this time the Brig had
displayed the Proud British flag and began for to play upon
us with her Stearn Chaser's but we took no notice of her
Shot but kept sweeping until the wind dying away and a
Smooth sea And we did not think it prudent for to sweep along
side not knowing what she was —— we took in our sweeps
and Cleared away for Action there Shot still flying over us
with British Glory we Spliced the Main Brace and then turned
too with Coolness we had gave her but three broadsides when
she gave us an Unlucky shot between wind and Water which
Obliedged us for to haul off as there was six feet of Water in
our hole and our Powder a Considerably damaged all hands
then turned too our pumps and we stopt the Leak in a few
Minuets our eneme was by this in a Crowd of sail Endeavouring to get clear of us but our Leak being stopt and we all
Taking a Stiff Dram we went to our sweeps and sweept
towards a Portuguese Brig who stood a Silent Spectator to our
Unpleasant play we Boarded her and took out Several Boxes
of Oranges and learnt by her that the Enemy was a Brig of
war Mounting fourteen Guns and Ninty Men we took in our
Boat and stowed her and then Opening the boxes we ate up
all the Oranges and then went to our sweeps again like hardy
tars and with a light breeze of wind we had the pleasure of
Being along of him by dark when we began our play again
and Continued it until ten at Night when it being very dark and
we could not See her but when she discharged her guns we
thought it best for to Leave of our play until daylight but
not forgetting to give her our Long two and thirty every half
hour until half past one in the Morning when it being our
Second Lieutenant's watch on deck and he not having a good
Lookout kept she Escaped Us the next Morning there being
several sail in sight We gave Chase to the one who was Most
suspected But she proved to be an Neutral then we Turned
too for to Mend our sails and Riging and the Carpenters in Re-
pairing the shot holes and as kind heavens would have it we
had no Employment for the doctor —— Nothing More
worth our Notice Until the eighteenth when the Man at the

Mast head discried a sail all hands was called to Make Sail in
Chase at eleven in the forenoon we Came Up with her she
proved to be an Irish Schooner With a Cargo of Provisions
Bound to Lisbon after Taking out our prisoners we put a
prize Master and Crew on Board and ordered her for the
United States the next day we boarded a neutral vessel and
put our prisoners on Board and wished them good Luck on
the ninth at one P M the Man at the mast gave Us the Joyful
cry of sail O but as the wind was Light We Made but little
progress in coming up to her at five in the afternoon we dispatched our Boat with the first Lieutenant and fourteen Men
well arm'd for to see what She Might be at half past Nine the
Boat Returned and gave us the Joyful Tidings that she was
a Brig under Sweedish Colours with a British Cargo of dry
goods and Jewlery from London Bound to Lisbon we lay by
her until the Next Morning then taking out our Prisoner's
we put a prize Master and Crew on Board of her and ordered
them for the United States on the Eleventh we Boarded an
Portuguese Brig and transported our prisoners of her nothing
More worth our Notice until the eighteenth when at two P M
as we was standing on the wind to the Southward and Eastward with a stiff Breeze we discovered a Brig Coming down
upon us with Studding sails below & Aloft we called all
hands to Quarters and we hoisted English Colours for to see
what she was But she soon had the english flag displayed at
her Main peak and began for to Make signals to Which Made
us suspect that she was a Brig of War But that did not Daunt
us for in a few Minuets we Was along side of him with our
English Colours still display'd at our Main Gaft as soon as
we was within hail of him we gave him a Broadside and
hoisted our Yankey flag at the Main topmast head when he
Returned us his Compliments by Giving us his Broad side
which did us no material Injury but on our giving him two
more Doses of our Yankey Pills he Was Obliedged for to
strike his Colours we Dispatched our Boat amediately on
Board of her which soon Returned Back and imformed us
that she was his British Majesty Packet Little Catharine from
falmouth Bound to the Brazils with dispatches but that they
had Drowned there Mail and that she was a considerably cut
in the Riging and hull and had one Man killed in the action
we then Boated our Prisoners with there dunage on Board

of us, the Little Catharine Mounted ten carriage guns and
thirty six Men she was a Beautiful New and Copper Bottom'd
Brig and a very fast sailer by the New's paper's that we found
in the prize it appears that the Brig that we fought on the
first of May was the Sir Frances Freeland a British Packet
Mounting fourteen gun's and had on Board at the Commence-
ment of the action Ninty six Men but by our good and well
directed shot we killed seventeen and wounded twenty five
and set her on fire three Several times which they Extin-
guished but she Having on Board two hundred and twenty
Thousand of Dollars in specia it made them fight much harder
then they would have done providing they had been in Ballast
she was towed into falmouth by a Frigate four day's after the
action where there Captain had a Sword presented to him
valued at one hundred Guineas for fighting so Boldly and the
Brig Was hauled up Unfit for any More Service ——— after
Receiving our prisoner on Board we put a Prize Master and
Crew on Board and ordered her for to Lay by us until it
Moderated so that we could Get out Provisions and Repair
her Rigging at day Light the next Morning the Man at the
Masthead Discovered a sail we gave chase to her with our
prize in Company on coming up with her she proved for to
be an portuguese Brig we soon transported our prisoners' on
Board of her and ordered her to Lisbon by the Prisoners
request, the sea runing So high we could do nothing with our
prize ——— the Next Morning it Moderating we took two
Brass nine pounder's and thirty Bushels of potatoes and then
ordered her for the first port in the United States Nothing
More occurd until the Ninth of June when the Man at Masthead Gave us the Joyful Tiding that there was a Strang sail
in sight all Hands was called for to Make sail in Chase and
we having a Stiff Breeze we was a long side of her in a short
time she proved for to be an Schooner Under Russian Colours
with a Cargo of Dry Goods and Brandy it being English Property we took our prisoners out and put a Prize Master and
Crew on Board and ordered her for the first Port in the United
States after taking out two Casks of Brandy the Man at Masthead discovered Another sail we amediately ordered the Prize
for to Make the best of her way in the Meantime we Called
all Hands for to Make sail in Chase and then Taking a Stiff
horn of Brandy both fore and aft We went to our Quarters
for to see who this Large ship Might be it being dark we ran

up Alongside without knowing what she was and gave her a
Broadside and finding she did not Return It We gave her two
More Doses and then Dispatch'd our Boat on Board of her
which soon Returned Back again and Imformed us that she was
an portuguese Ship in Ballast from Madeira Bound to Lisbon
After a strict overhauling we permitted her to procede While
we enjoyed another Drop of Brandy the Fruits of our Labour
Nothing more Worth noticing Until the seventeenth of June
when at daylight We discovered a Large schooner to Windward of Us standing on the Wind as soon as they perceived
us they Bore up we ameditately called All hands to Quarters
Expecting for to have a Dust with her she coming down upon
us with all Sail set and a Beautiful Breeze and we perceived
that he had the British flag displayd we Shortned Sail for to
receive him as soon as he was within Gun shot we let him
have a Broad side which cut away his topsail Halyards then
he rounded too and we gave him two More Broadsides when
he Doused his mainsail as he had his Colours Sewed on the
Leach of his mainsail expecting for to frighten us but he
found his Mistake we Amediately dispatched our Boat on
Board of her which soon Returned back and Imformed us
that she was the English Merchant schooner John from Barbadoes Bound to Lisbon in Ballast and there Captain drinking
too freely that Morning he thought himself on Board of A
Frigate and he said to his Crew that he could take a Yanky
Privateer without firing a gun but alas how soon the Case
was altered for Myself with three More Went into his Cabin
and draged him from his Cot and Tumbled him into the Boat
without either hat Coat or Shoes on and Transported him on
Board of the Privateer with the Remainder of his Crew then
We onbent his Sails and sent them on Board of us then we
set fire to her and Left her to the Mercy of the Waves and
Flames our privateer by this time getting foul we thought it
Most prudent for to Make the best of our way home on the
twenty fifth we touched at Santa Crista for Water And Fresh
provisions after receiving forty Hogsheads of Water sixty
Bushels of potatoes six sheep and three Bullocks we took our
departure on the Thirtyeth we Boarded a Portuguese ship
from Lisbon Bound to the Brazils with provisions we took out
thirty Barrels of Bread and one Barrel of hams we paid for
them in the Bill of Exchange that we took out of the Portuguese Brig but he Might as Well have had the Leaf of an

old Almanack as the Bill of Exchange, for there payment was stopt ——— but as he thought himself well paid we had no Occasion to think hard nothing more until the fourth of July in the Morning it being Moderate and very foggy we took in all sail for to Celebrate the day at Eleven in the forenoon all Hands was called for to Splice the Main Brace at Noon we fired a salute of seventeen guns and then we went to drinking the Remainder of the Day Nothing More occurd until the first of August when the Man at Masthead discovered a Sail all Hands was then called aft for to see if they was Willing for to go in chase but we being eager for to Improve our Oppertunity not knowing how Soon that we might have our Liberty taken from Us we Replied that we would see her by all means in a few Minuets we was in a Cloud of Sail but as the Wind was light we did not Reach her that Night, at daylight the next Morning she being About three miles dist[t.] from us we Man'd out our Boat with our First Lieutenant Myself and ten Men well arm'd for to see what she was on Boarding her she proved for to be an English Brig from Halifax Bound to the west India with A Cargo of Fish and Lumber after taking out the prisoners we put a prize Master and Crew and ordered her for the first port in the United States Nothing more worth our Noticeing here Until the ninth ins[t.] when the Man at the Mast head discovered a sail all hands was Called for to Make sail in Chase at two in the Afternoon we got near enough for to see that she was a schooner at three the Wind freshening we Carryed away our fore gaft but we soon had it repaird and Renewed the Chase at four we gave him a Gun and hoisted English Colours but they refusing to show there Colours We ran up alongside of him and gave him three Broadsides for not showing his Colours we Dispatched our Boat on Board of him and Conveyed there Captain on Board of us, on Enquiring the Reason of his not showing his Colours he replyd that he had two sets of Colours and he did Not know which one for to hoist he said That he was from Anaplis Nova Scotia bound to the West India with a Cargo of fish and Lumber after taking out the prisoners we put A prize Master and Crew on Board and ordered her for the first port in the United States We then kept on our Course in great hopes of getting on shore to our Native Land but alas our hopes was at an end for on the fifteenth of August at day light in the Morning we discovered two Frigate's within three gun shots of Us we soon had all hands Up and crowded all sail but our enemy was in a Cloud of sail in a few Minuets and soon Comme[n]ced firing with there Bow Chasers upon us but to no purpose until one of them out sailing the other came up with us so that her Shot Reached us then we began for to play upon her with our stern Chasers until she came with in Musquet Shot then seing that we could not get Clear our Captain thus addrest us— Men younow See that we cannot get Clear of our enemy I hope that you will stick to your Quarters and if they give us but One gun after our Colours is doust we will run them Up again and fight until we sink a long side of them then giving our Noble Commander three Huzza's we ceased firing and doused our Colours to our great Mortification then we went below for to pack up our Dunage but we was soon Hurryed into the boats for the Enemy to take Command of the Herald of Seventeen Carriage guns we was carryed on Board of the Armied Frigate fifty four in Number of us and then one half was transported on Board of the Endymon Frigate they Man'd the privateer and ordered her for Halifax then the Frigates Stood in for Marthas Vinyard on the next day they Captured the Invincible Napoleon after a Cruise of sixty day's from Charleston Bound into New York but those fatal Devils (the English) put an end to there as well as our Carier that Evening they fell in with the Majestic razea Bound to the Chesapeak who ordered the two Frigates to Halifax where we arrived on the twenty second and on the twenty fourth we was Conveyed to prison on Melville Island* there i found Mr. Samuel Cook our first Mate When we left Boston in the Monkey W Edwards and several other Salem Men here i was Imformed of My Brother Samuels Death, and that all the Young people in salem was Married or Expected to be on the seventeeth of september Josiah Gwinn and William Gray received Letters from Salem There was one also came for Samuel Lambert but as he was put out in the first prize I took his Letter under my Care and thought that the Lord has not forgot Me if My Friends has for he has put a Letter into My hand's altho' it was not Sent to Me i took full as much pleasure in readin[g] it and if i should fall in with him it would Be a great satisfaction for him to hear from home on the twenty first of September the Crew of the Ida of Boston was Marched here, I Learnt by Mr Enos Knowlton of Salem that My Parents Brothers and Sister was in good Health when he Left home that was on the third of June and that My Brother George lived in Lynn this was the first time that i have heard From My Parents since i Left home it Being now Nine Months he also Imformed Me that those Let-

---

*See letter, page 29.

ters that i sent on From Charleston S C all went safe home—here prisoners was coming in dayly while a Great Number paid the debt of Nature and went to there Long home we Made this our home Until the twenty seventh when two hundred and Fifty of us was transported on Board of the Akbar Frigate for England here we was confin'd in her hole where we could have no Light nor Enjoy the Wholesome air but in darkness we Was Obliedged to Lay both' Day and Night for We had not Highth enough for to set on our Back Sides but to eat Drink and sleep we Must Lay too it i had been in this Situation but a few day's with my Fellow Prisoners when I was taken down Sick with a Slow Fever and in the Course of one week there was fifty Seven taken down with the same Deseas and every day there was More or Less paid the debt of Nature no Tender Mother for to Nurse them no Friends nor Relation to Mourn for them and no acquaintance for to Shed Tears When my Messmates would come and tell Me that a Nother was Just Launched to there Watery Tomb I did certainly Expect for to be the next But it pleased the Lord that I should Recover My Health again on the twenty seventh we Discovered the Land and on the twenty ninth We arived at Plymouth Eng$^{d.}$ as soon as we came to Anchor i had the Privalige of Purchasing some Bread Butter and Milk and Fruit Which finly Reviv'd Me on the thirty first of October we was Landed in plymouth and Marched to dartmoor it being about sixteen Miles in the Country and the Roads Exceeding bad and the Most was Without shoes or stockings and the Soldiers pricking us up with there Bayonets thus we poor half Starv'd prisoners was Marched in the Rain from seven in the Morning until half past Eight in the Evening without having one Morsel to eat and cast into a dark Cold and Wet Prison without having where with all to eat or rest our weary Limbs upon thus we Was Locked up for to spend a Cold and disagreable Night in the Morning there Clerk Entered With a Band of soldiers for to take the highth's Complection's and where we was born and then turned us Into the Yard for to Receive hammocks beds and Blankets that was as full of Lice as the Devil is of Wickedness but howasever those did not frighten us after taking Breakfast I took a Walk round the Prison's and here i found our First prizes Crew that had been here three Months and I gave Samuel Lambert his Letter I also found here Confind in these prisons Four thousands and five Hundred American's for to Lement there dismal Situation and amongst them there was five hundred Salem Men this Was the first time that ever i found all Salem together after dinner i thought on getting in to some prison for to hang up my Hammoc after walking round some time i took up my Lodgings in Number seven prison for to pass A Cold and tegeous Winter—Now i will give the discriptions of those prison's as Near as i can firstly—there is seven prison's that stands in a Circular form, each of them large enough for to Contain eighteen hundred Men, Number four or the Middle prison is for the Blacks in which there is Schools kept of all Descriptions such as Dancing Fencing Boxing and Music schools—Secondly— on the top of a Mountain where the Clouds ranges the ground these prison's are pitch where it Must be on a very Clear day that we can see from one prison to the other, the First Month that I had the pleasure of being in these palaces we never had sight of the sun but three different times and nothing but a continual rain from the first of November to the first of January— Thirdly—these prison's is an Excilent school for all those that had Led an Irregular Life for all those that has been given to Drunkardness here before, they have time dayly for to Realise there past Conduct and to see the fruits of hard drinking for it Brings on all kinds of Bad Vices such as Idleness Lazyness Thieving and at Last the[y] Commit a Murder which puts an end to there Lives. Fourthly—to those that never knew the Value of Money will Learn by Living here how to be Saving and frugal for the time to Come, here they can see that some that has been saving and has had Money when they came into these prisons can with there scanty allowance and a Little Money Live very Comfortable, while those that had Money when they had there Liberty would stay on Shore Until every Cent was gone and then would be Obliedged for to put to sea again without a penny for to help them selves and then they would get Captured by there enemy and sent to this place and the first thing that they would do would be for to sell off what few Clothes they had and then they would be 'tempted by the help of the Devil for to steal from there Mess Mates and Fellow prisoner's and then there backs would be Brought to disgrace and there eyes open'd, then they would see wherein they had been wrong, thus we May see that a prison although it is a place of Confinment it is the best School that ever Man or Boy went into, if they will but give heade to what they hear and see—Fifthly a person in these prisons should take great Care of his health for in taking cold's it Creates a bad Cough and hoarsness and then if he goes into the Hospital he at first is put into a Cold Bath and then he is Bled as long as he has a drop of Blood in his Veins, I knew a Man that went into the hospital with a Bad cold and he at the first Bleeding had two hundred and forty ounces of Blood taken from him, the doctors here Makes a practice of Bleeding a person as long as he has Breath to draw—

Now i shall go on with My dayly Observations

November the first i spent the day in Company with My acquaintanc and seeing the Fashons, On the second i finding Myself Very unwell i kept My house and was Visited by Joseph Pitman of Salem

On the third i remained in Much the same state of Health i was visited by several of My Acquaintanc who advised me for to see the Doctor On the fourth i perceiving My Cold Increasing I went into the Hospital for Advice from the Doctor he gave Me a dose of Phisic with Which i am in hope's for to get Relief

On the fifth i found but Little Relief From my Phisic in the fore part of the day I took a Walk out for to see My Acquaintance in the after Noon it being wet i kept My house

On the sixth i was visited by several Salem Men where i passed the day very Comfortably

On the seventh i perceived My health Much recovered i made a visit into N° one prison

On the eighth it being wet and Disagreable Weather i kept house and passed the [time] In Company with Mr Israel Phippen and William Ashton of Salem Mass ——

On the Ninth I Made a tour over to Number one and three prison's and returned again At noon and kept house the remainder of the day ——

On the tenth we had two hundred Fellow Prisoners arrive here from Chatham in which was the following Salem men R Wiggins W Abbott and John Beckford and John Fisher

On the Eleventh i was visited by Joseph Pitman and William Garret and the Evening i passed in Company with J Phippen

On the twelfth i made a tour over to Number three prison in Company With P W Pinder and E Perkins

On the Thirteenth i kept House during the day and the Evening was passed in Company with Mr Felt and Daniel Very

On the fourteenth i passed the Day in Writing and the Evening in Company With Josiah Gwinn and Joseph Millet

On the fifteenth I Made a tour over to Number one and three prisons in Company with Samuel Lambert

On the sixteenth I was Visited by John Ingersol of Salem
on the Seventeeth I passed the day and evening at home in company with E A Porter

On the Eighteenth i Made a tour over to Number one prison with Josiah Gwinn in Company and in the evening i was Visited by Mr William Ashton and W Richardson

On the Ninteenth I passed the day in Company with Josiah Orne and J Snow

On the Twentyeth I Made a tour Into Number four Prison for to see two Black Men Flog'd for Stealing from there Fellow Prisoners I passed the evening with John Phippen

On the twenty first I Made a tour through Number Five prison for the first time and in the Evening i was favoured with the Company of Mrss Israel and John Phippen and Samuel Shepherd

On the twenty second i Made a visit through Number one and three prison's in Company With Mrss Samuel and Charles Green of Salem

On the twenty third i kept house and had Several of My Acquaintanc to Visit Me

On the twenty fourth I passed the Day in Writing and the evening was spent in Company with E A Porter Samuel Archer And William Richardson of Salem

On the twenty fifth I passed the fore part Of the day in Company with Joseph Pitman in the afternoon we had a small draft of Eleven Men Arrive here from Plymouth, No Salem Men

On the twenty sixth I passed the fore part of the day in Number four prison in Company With Nathaniel Silsby and Edward Gale

On the twenty seventh i Made a Visit Into Number five prison in Company with Messrs Wigging and Upton and Nehemiah Butman

On the twenty eighth I wore away the fore part of the day in writing and in the afternoon amongst My Friends in talking About the Salem Girls &c.

On the twenty Ninth in the Morning I Made a Tour through All the prisons and in the Afternoon and Evening in Company with J Gwinn

On the thirtyeth I Received a Visit from Samuel Lambert and Joseph Pitman and in the Evening I was in Company with S Archer

December the first I kept My house and Wrote during the day and the Evening In Company with Mr Felt of Salem

On the Second I took Breakfast With Messrs Niel and Strout and the Remainder of the day in Reading

On the third I kept My house and was Visited by Mr Upton and the Evening was spent in Company with Samuel Shepherd

On the fourth I went into Number four Prison for to see the Fashons and pass the time

On the Fifth I was at the Trial of our Cook's during the day and late in the Evening the Jury Brought in there Verdict Guilty of Robbing there Fellow Prisoner's of there Small Allowance and Skimming the fat from of the Soup they was Sentenced for to Receive Eighteen Lashes each on there Naked back As an Example for others

On the Sixth I paid a Visit to P W Pinder and Elijah Perkins of Salem

On the Seventh I kept My house and Was favoured with the Company of Daniel Very and the Evening in Company with John Phippen

On the Eighth I Made a Visit into Number five prison and past a few hour's in Company with John Beckford of Salem

On the Ninth I went to see two Young Boy's Floged for Stealing a Pound Note From there Mess Mates they Received two Dozen each on there Naked Backs Not for Stealing, but for being Cought

On the tenth I Made a tour through Number four prison for to pass a dull and Tegeous hour and the Evening in Company with Samuel Shepherd and William Felt

On the Eleventh I Made a Visit over to Number one and three prisons in Company with Josiah Orne and James Snow

On the Twelfth I went into Number five prison for to see John Taylor Junr the Son of Captain John Taylor of New York Who had hung himself During the Night

May the Lord be with him and the Devil Miss him

On the thirteenth I kept My house and Was Visited by James Harrison and E Gale

On the fourteenth I Made a Tour through all the prisons' for to pass a way the Tegeous time which goes heavily here In Confinement the Evening with W Ashton

On the fifteenth I Made a Visit to Joseph Pitman and John Chadwick

On the sixteenth I Made a Visit over to Number four for to see the Fashons

On the Seventeeth I kept My House and Received Company as they Came

On the Eighteenth I Made a tour through Number one three prisons' in Company with Mr Robertson and Josiah Orne of Salem

On the Nineteeth I made a Tower through Number five Prison for to see My Acquaintanc

On the twentyeth I kept My house and spent the day in writing and the Evening in Company with John Phippen

On the twenty first I Made a Tour through Number four for to see the fashons and to hear the New's of the day of which we have a plenty of about this time

On the twenty second I Made a Visit Into Number five prison in Company with John Beckford and Richard wiggins of Salem

On the twenty third I kept My house after taking My Morning walk and Was visited by Mr Isreal Phippen of Salem

On the twenty fourth I past the Day in Company with Joseph Pitman in talking about the pleasure's of Salem

On the twenty fifth i past the day in writing and the Evening with Mr Eulin of Salem

On the twenty sixth I Made a Tour through Number one three and five prisons for to See my Acquaintanc and hear the News

On the twenty seventh I was visited by Mr Samuel Green and John Millet

On the twenty eighth we had a Draft of four hundred and fifty arrive here from Halifax and the Cape of Good hope amongst them was the Crew of the General Putman Privateer of Salem Chiefly Salem men

On the twenty Ninth i was in Company with William Boden of Salem

On the thirtyeth I kept My house and Received Company as it came both^e good and bad

On the thirty first I made a Visit Over to Number one and was Imformed that the Preliminaries of Peace was signd on the twenty fourth Ins^t between the United States and Great Briton which was a Joyful News

January the first 1815 we had the American flag display'd on each of the prison's and then with three hearty Huzzas We Congratulated each other and then we passt the day in talking of home

On the Second I kept My house and pass'd the day in writing &c &c &c

On the third I was at the trial of William Shute for Stealing a Watch from One of his messmates the Jury after being Out for one hour Brought in there Virdict that the Prisoner was Guilty and Sentancet him to Receive thirty six Lashes on his Naked Back for to teach him better the Next time

On the fourth I Made a Visit to Mr Samuel Shepherd and William Ashton and the Evening in Company with S Archer

On the fifth I being a little Lame I kept My house and was Visited by a Number Of My acquaintance two Numerous to Mention.

On the Sixth I was Visited by Joseph Pitman and P W Pinder who Imformed Me that My old Ship mate Daniel Appleton had departed this Life by the Small Pox

On the seventh I Yet Remaining Lame I kept my house in the Afternoon We had a Small draft of thirty Men came Up from Plymouth Chiefly Salem Men the Next that Comes will be Blind George the Cryer

On the eighth I finding Myself Very Unwell I kept My Bed and Received no Company

On the Ninth I Remained in Much the Same State of Illness—

On the tenth I perceiving My Self A Little better I took My regular walk round the prisons in Company with E A Porter

On the Eleventh I kept My house and was in Company with Joshua Strout

On the twelfth in the afternoon One of the Missionary Ministers Came into N° four Prison for to preach to the Prisoners

On the thirteenth the Court Sat on A Young Man for Stealing a Great Coat he Was Sentanced to Receive four Dozen of Lashes on his Naked Back but after Receiving twenty Six he fainted away which Caused him for to be Released for another Oppertunity

On the fourteenth I Made a Tour through Number one three and five prison's for to See My Acquaintance

On the fifteenth this Morning I Was Imformed that Mr Daniel Archer of Salem had departed this Life in the hospital

On the Sixteenth I kept house and Was Visited by J Orene J Strout J Snow and Several others too Numerous to Mention

On the seventeenth in the Morning I Made a Visit to N° four prison and the afternoon I went over to Number one prison for to see a fellow prisoner have two Large Letters put into his Cheeks for being a Traitor to his Country and damning the flag

On the Eighteenth after taking My Morning walk i was visited by J Orne also a small draft arrived here from Plymouth

On the Ninteeth In the fore part of the day I kept house and in the Afternoon I Made a Visit into N° four

On the twentyeth I passed the day in Writing and the Evening in Company with D Very

On the twenty first we had our Market Stopt on Account of three Men of this prison taking down the Window Shetters of N° Six prison and Making tables of them

On the twenty second the Prisoner's of N° one three four & five Prison's Sent a Letter into our, or N° seven Prison, to Imform Us that if we did Not deliver up those three Men to Capt Shortland that they would Come and take him by force but without waiting for an answer at two in the afternoon there was sixteen hundred Men assembled and Came into this prison and took the Men by force and delivered them up to Capt Shorland and the Cashot brought them Up

On the twenty third we had our Market open'd and in the Afternoon I Made a Tour through N° one three & four prisons In Company with Josiah Gwinn of Salem and Several More of My Acquaintanc

On the twenty fourth I kept My house and was Visited by Joseph Pitman

On the twenty fifth I Made a Visit to Josiah Orne and James Snow

On the twenty Sixth in My Morning Walk I was Imformed of the Death of Mr Daniel Very of Salem who Departed this Life Last Evening in the Hospital, In the Afternoon I received My Monthly Pay of Six Shillings and Eight pence

On the twenty Seventh I kept My house and was Visited by Joseph Millet

On the twenty Eighth I past the day in Company with Josiah Gwinn & William Ashton

On the twenty Ninth it being on Sunday i went into N° four Prison for to hear the Black Preacher and to My Great Surprise I saw Joseph Pitman on his Humble knee's Offering up his prayers to his Almighty God

On the thirtyeth in the Afternoon I was Visited by P W Pinder who Imformed Me that James Snow and Joseph Pitman had been taken into the Black Society Likewise they had moved there Bags & hammocks into the Black Prison

On the Thirtyeth first this Morning Josiah Gwinn went into the Hospital with the Small Pox and I am fearful that he Will

End his days in this place as the Small pox Rages Very Rapid, I was Imformed that Seven poor Souls Departed this Life Last Night

February the First I kept house and Was Visited by Josiah Orne and William Gray but Could hear Nothing from My Old Friend

On the Second I Made a Tour through N° one three and four Prison's in Company with Mr Gray in the Afternoon the Doctors from the Hospital Made a Visit through all the prison's and desird all those that Never had the Small Pox for to be Noculated for to prevent this Infectious Disorder from Raging farther In the Afternoon I went into N° four Prison for to hear the Word of God Preached by a White Minister from Plymouth

On the third Early in the Morning A Jury of Doctors came for to Examine the prison's and Found the air for to be Nine Degrees warmer on the Middle Deck than out of Doors and fifteen on the Upper Deck

On the fourth this Morning I Received A Letter from the doctors assistant to Imform Me that My Old Friend Josiah Gwinn was very Low and dangerously Sick ——— late in the Afternoon we had the prize Crew of the Privateer Brutus Arive here — one More Salem Man· by the Name of Swaysey

on the fifth in the Morning I Visited Josiah Orne and in the Afternoon I went to Meeting in Number four Prison In Company with Samuel Archer and James Harrison of Salem

On the Sixth I took a tour through N° four Prison in Company with P W Pinder

On the Seventh In My Morning Walk I was Imformed that Mr Robert Adams of our Privateer had departed this Life last Evening in the hospital — but nothing from J Gwin

On the Eighth this Morning E A Porter went into the hospital from our Mess in the Afternoon I Received a Visit from Capt Josiah Orne of Salem

on the Ninth in the fore part of the day I past in Reading in the afternoon to Meeting

On the tenth I past the day in Writing and the Evening in Company with Mr John Phippen and W Ashton

On the Eleventh I passed the fore part of the day in Company with Wm Gray in the afternoon I Received a Letter from Mr Edward A Porter who Inform's me that Josiah Gwinn is very dangerously Sick

On the twelfth early this Morning I Received a letter from Mr Wm Young he Imforms me that Josiah Gwinn is past all hope's of Recovery Likwise desirded that if I wished for to have him Laid out decent for to have a Shirt and handkerchief sent in —— I Imediately sent him a White Shirt and handkerch[ief]

On the thirteenth I passed the fore part of the day in Company with M^r I phippen And M^r price in the Afternoon with J Pitman and James Snow of Salem

On the fourteenth we had our Market stopt for Refusing to Deliver up the prize Master of the Vivid—he for Attempting for to Blow his Vessel up at Sea has been In Solitary Confinment for ten Months and Last Sunday he Made his Escape from the Cashot And came into our prison this Morning Captn Shortland sent in a Letter to Imform us that If we did not give him up that he would stop the Market and all Intercourse with the other prison's to which we Refused to Comply With——in the fore part of the day when the Lamp lighters came in for to trim there Lamps we Seized them and took there Oil from them and hove their Ladders over the Wall—soon after the Man that takes the filth out of the Prison Yards Came in with his Cart and two horses we Imediately Seized him and turned the horses out again —and then Sent a letter to Captn Shortland to Inform him that there Should not be one Man go out Side of the Prison Walls to work for him— Early in the Afternoon he sent two hundred Soldiers for to turn us into the prisons they Were drawn up in a Line with Loaded Musquets and done there best for to get us in but all In vain they then Received a Reinforcment of four hundred More and drove us round the Prison's three or four times and then we told them that if they would take the Soldiers up to the gate and for to order arms and then we would go in peacably to which they Consent'd and after they had drawn there Soldiers away from the Prison doors, we had a Reinforcment of one thousand Men from our prison and then we told them that we would not go in until Night they then Ordered there Soldiers home and we Gave them three hearty cheers and kept the Liberty of the Yard until Sundown to the Great Mortification of the British officers & Soldier's

On the fifteenth I past in writing but could hear Nothing from My Friend Mr Gwinn

On the sixteenth I past the day in Company with Wm Gray at noon I received a Letter from M^r W^m. Young he Inform's me that my friend Mr Gwinn is little better

On the seventeenth in the afternoon I went for to see two of My Fellow Prisoners flog'd for Stealing they Received one dozen each on there Naked Back

On the Eighteenth I past my Morning walk in Company with Wm Gray in the afternoon I was Imformed that My Friend Mr Gwinn has not seen out of his Eyes this fifteen days past

On the Ninteenth I made a Visit into N° five Prison in Company with P W Pinder in the afternoon we had a draft of Eighty Men arrive here

On the twentyeth in the Morning we had Reported in the New's papers that the U S Frigate President was Captured In the afternoon I Received a Letter from Mr Young he Imform's me that My friend Mr Gwinn remains much the same only he has Lost his left Eye, in the Evening i past in writing

On the twenty first I past the fore part of the day in Writing in the afternoon I made a tour through N° one three four and five Prisons

on the twenty second at day light this Morning We had the American Flag display'd on Each of the Prisons in Memory of the Immortal Washington it being his birth day at noon i received the sad tidings of the Death of my Friend Josiah Gwinn Aged twenty two he died this Morning at Nine O clock after a Shocking and Painful Sickness of twenty three days

On the twenty third I past the fore part of the day in Company with Joseph Pitman and the afternoon in Company with John Phippen H Upton and Mr Eulin of Salem in the Evening the Jury was Called together for to try a Man for Stealing he was found Guilty and Sentanced him to receive one hundred of fifty Lashes on his Naked Back

On the twenty fourth I past the fore part of the day in Reading in the afternoon I was Visited by Josiah Orne and John Phippen of Salem

On the twenty fifth in the Morning I Made a Tour through N° one three & four Prison's in Company with Wm Gray in the afternoon George Mansfield of Salem went into the hospital with the Small pox

On the twenty Sixth it being on Sunday I went to Meeting in N° four Prison in the Evening I past in Reading—Time goes Tegeous.

On the twenty Seventh I past the fore part of the day in Company with Joseph Millet and Wm Ashton

On the twenty Eighth in the fore part of the day i past in Company with P W Pinder and the afternoon in writing so ends February

March th[e] 1 I past in Meditating on the Deaths of so many of My Fellow Prisoners

on the Second at Noon Edward A Porter Came out of the hospital in the afternoon I went for to hear the Rev Mr Jones Preach in N° four Yard he is, a White Preacher from Plymouth he Makes us a Visit Every thursday

On the third I received My Monthly pay of six Shillings and eight pence in the afternoon we had one Hundred and fifty fellow prisoners added to our Number There is at this present time Upwards of six Thousand Men here

On the fourth I past the day in writing

On the fifth in the forenoon I went to Meeting in the afternoon John Mack of Salem Made Me a visit and requested that i would let him have a suit of his Cousin's Clothes and I seeing that he was Quite destitute of Clothing I Let him have one Jacket & Trousers one Shirt and one pair of Stockings for which he promises Me that he will Satisfy his Uncle Gwinn on his Arival in Salem.

On the Sixth I was visited by Josiah Orne in the afternoon i Made a tour through N° one three four and five prison's in Company with Wm Gray

On the Seventh I past the day in writing in the afternoon we had a draft of fifty American prisoners Arrive hear part of the U S Brig Syren Crew

On the Eighth I past the day in writing in the afternoon I received a Short visit from P W Pinder

On the Ninth I was Visited by Josiah Orne In the Afternoon I made a Tour through N° four Prison in Company with E A Porter and several other Salem men

On the Tenth I past the day in writing and the Evening in Company with Wm Ashton and S Sheppard

On the Eleventh in the fore noon i was Visited by Josiah Orne in the afternoon i was visited by John Phippen we had the Accounts in to day's Paper of the defeat of the British army at New Orleans

On the twelfth I past the day i Cannot tell My Readers how for the time goes much more Tegeous now then it did before we had the New's of Peace it is sixty Nine days since the favourite Sloop of war sailed for America with the dispatches—and no New's yet

On the thirteenth, altogether or Charity My Readers I presume that some of you who never has been in Confinment may suppose that a prisoner of War cannot assist a person in distress and that has there Sweet Liberty, but i will tell you to the Contrary for Last week one of the Assistance by the Name of Paul he had the Care of a Man that was derange'd in the hospital and Last Wednesday he called Mr Paul to his bed side for to speak with him and awhilst they was a talking this devils Bird Stabbed Mr Paul in the heart and a Nother young man Came to his assistance was served the same but Mr Paul died amediately and has Left a wife and several small Children to bemoan his sad fait — and to day it was proposed that we his remaining fellow priseners should on Next tuesday give the widow Paul the Money that should be laid out for our fish and potatoes which will amount to three hundred Dollars and for us to fast on that day

Mr Paul was an American Born but Married in England and his Wife had followed him to A small Town hard by that she Might assist her husband to the Necessity of Life

On the thirteenth in the fore Noon I was Visited by Josiah Orne and Mr Robertson in the afternoon I made a Visit to P W Pinder and Joseph Pitman

On the fourteenth in the fore part of the day i past in reading in the afternoon i made a Visit to I Phippen it was reported this afternoon that the Favourite sloop of war had Arived but I put no confidence in it as we have had such Reports frequently for this some time past but I hope that the time will soon come when I shall see us poor Lousy set going out of these Iron Gates and to Return to our Native home and once more Embrace our Blessed Liberty

On the fifteenth in the fore part of the day i past in reading in the afternoon i was visited by Joseph Pitman who requested that I would lend him a Little Money until he got home I let him have four Dollars in the afternoon we had the accounts of the Favourite sloop of war arriving with dispatches from America the Contents is not yet made known

On the sixteenth we had the American Flag display'd at sun rise it was on this Blessed morning that we had the news of peace for a Certainty and in the evening we had the prison's Illuminated for the Glorious News that we have Received

On the seventeenth i was as ill Natured as the devil all day with the worst of pain Called the tooth Ache but wrongly Named

On the Eighteenth in the fore part of day i was visited by Sam¹ Green in the afternoon i made a visit into N° three prison to P W Pinder in Company with Joseph Pitman this morning we dispatched a Letter of to London to Mr Beasly the Agent for American Prisoners for to Inform him that it was Peace between the United States & Great Briton

On the Ninteenth in the fore noon i was Visited by Mr Samuel Cook who Requested that I would let him have one Guinea until his arrival at home to which I Generously Did knowing that he was in want of it in the Evening we went to bed soon as I was up until daylight this Morning in Company with Isreal phippen on Buisinize of Importance

On the twentyeth I was taken very ill and was Obliedged for to take to my bed, at Noon M^r I Phippen prepar'd a pot of strong wormwood Tea and Insisted of my taking it and in the Evening prepared Me the Second dose this afternoon there was forty Men Called out for to go to France for to Join some American ships

On the twenty first i turned out inflicted with the tooth ache i went into the Receiving house with the Intent to have it taken out, but not liking the looks of the doctors mate i turned short round and came out and went into N° one prison and had three of my Jaw teeth taken out by a fellow prisoner this Evening i find myself very weak having had no appetite this weak past but i am in hopes to wear it of

On the twenty second in the fore part of the day i was Visited by Samuel Cook and Wm Ashton at noon Edward A Porter Received a Letter from his Affectionate Mother in Salem dated Decr 14th Last Evening Wm Story a ship mate of Mine endeavoured for to make his Escape but was caught and Confind in the Cashot

On the twenty third i past in writing and was visited by several of my Friends but could not Receive them I find my Health restord again

On the twenty fourth in the fore part of the day i was visited by Samuel Shepherd and Isreal Phippen

What must be the anxious feelings of our tender parents

twenty fifth we have the accounts in to day's paper of Bonaparte's arriving into parris and King Lewis had made his Escape — at Noon we had the Effigy of Mr Beasly hung and then Burnt for his kind attention to the American prisoners of war on the twenty sixth i past the fore part of the day in Company with Wm Gray and the Evening in Company with S Cook and I phippen   On Anxiety of Mind Last sunday Evening I did Certainly expect for to be out of these prisons before now but i am disappointed my hopes is all but Exhausted My patience is all gone but alas if we are anxious Thoughts of our parents Friends and Relations

On the twenty Seventh in the fore part of the day i past in Reading in the afternoon in Company With George Felt and John Ingersoll of Salem

On the twenty Eighth i past the fore part of the day in company with Wm Gray in the afternoon I was Visited by Josiah Orne and Samuel Cook

On the twenty Ninth i past the day in Reading and the Evening in Company with S Cook S Shepperd and Mr Eulin and I phippen

On the thirtyeth I made a Tour through N° one and three prison's and the Evening i past in Company with Israel phippen and C Gotier

On the thirty first i Received A Visit from J Orne and Wm Gray and past the Evening with Wm Ashton

April the first presented it self with uncommon pleasant weather in the fore noon i Received a Visit from Mr Henry Allen who requested that I would let him have a few pounds as all the Officers of the privateer that he was Captured in was to be Detained and he wished for to make his Escape if possible But i could not make it Convenient at pressent as i having purchased several prize Tickets in the private Armed Schoone Herald of New York but i felt very Sorry that i could not assist him in the Evening i past in Company with Samuel Cook and S Shepherd

On the second i past the day in reading & the evening in company with Edward A Porter

On the third i received a Visit from Mr Josiah Orne and Peter Washington Pinder

On the fourth this Morning there was twelve hundred Letters arived here from America Chiefly from Marblehead and Salem but none for Myself but i hope that it May please the almighty God for to spare me that i may once more see My parents and know the reason for there Slighting me so much as they have done since I left Salem .

On the fifth i past the fore part of the day in Writing in the afternoon in Company with Wm Gray

On the sixth day of April as the prisoner of N° five and seven Prisons made a Small hole in the wall near the Barracks when Captn Shortland gave Orders for the Soldiers to fire in upon the Unarmed Prisoners and a Dreadful Massacree took place in the first place he sent the Turnkeys for to Lock three of the doors out of four so that Escape to the prison's was Impossible and after we had got Mostly in at the Remaining door and those that was at the lower ends of the yard and knew nothing of the Disturbance was mostly killed or wounded—in N° one and three where there was no offence given and without any provication they fired and then Charged Bayonet Many were killed and wounded in this yard and to Compleat the scene of slaughter and death a Simeler Scein took place in N° 4 Yard it appears that the Blacks were near the gates of there Yard Gamboling and not Mistrusting any harm when a dreadful fire from the top of the wall killed several and wounded many the Soldiers kept a Cross fire upon the only Remaining door that we had open—so that it was Impossible for any to Escape i have not yet Received the true list of the killed and wounded

On the seventh as soon as it was daylight i went round for to view the yards i found a Consider Blood in our yard and in N° four but not so much in N° one at 10 in the four noon i Received the List of the Killed and wounded, but thanks be to God there was but seven Killed and fifty wounded and the Most of them has lost there Legs or there arms and several Mortally wounded—I Cannot but help Remarking the fait of one Young Man—after he was wounded and Making the Best of his way for the prison five of the British Soldiers came up with him and and put there Musquets to his head and Blow'd his Brains out a gainst the wall

on the Eighth i was visited by J Orne who imforms me that there is a Number of Prisoners Missing supposed to have been Massacred on the 6 Ins and Buryed by the Soldiers

on the Ninth i was Visited by J Orne and G Felt in the evening i past in Company with I Phippen and S Cook

on the Tenth in the fore noon i was Visited by S Cook and Wm Ashton

On the Eleventh i past the day in Writing but no Glad Tidings do we hear yet no prospect of ever seeing our native home again

on the twelfth i past the fore part of the day in Company with Wm Abbot and Henry Upton and the Latter part in Meditating

On the thirteenth i past the day in writing
On the Fourteenth i past the day in Reading
On the fifteenth i past in Company with William Gray and the Sixteenth it Being Sunday I past the day in Meditating on our unhappy Situation
On the Seventeeth in the fore noon I was Visited by Josiah Orne and the afternoon by Mr Samuel Green and J Pickman of Salem
On the Eighteenth I past in Reading
On the Nineteeth O happy day hath though at length arrived our hearts Leap for Joy at the Glad tidings that we do hear— My Gentle Readers i will not keep you in Suspence any Longer for the News that we are Rejoiced at is that we had a Draft of two hundred and fifty Men taken from us for to Join a Cartel and proceed to there Native home and the Blessed Land of Liberty and once more Enjoy the Company of there tender wives and Children Parents and Relations but for our Sweet Hearts we can put no dependence in them any Longer than we are with them for there hearts is fickel and there Minds Changes as the wind.—
On the twentyeth i past the fore part of the day in Company with E A Porter
On the twenty first I past the day in writing and Received Several Visits from My Acquaintanc too Numeras to Mention
On the twenty second i past the day in Sorrow and vexation and Cursing those that is the Cause of our Confinment at this time
On the twenty third i past in Reading Religious Books (at intervals)
on the twenty fourth we had a draft of four hundred and fifty men called out for to Join a Cartel—but my Patience is so much Exhausted and My health in a declining fast that i shall Endeavour for to purchase a Turn in the next Draft that goes from here
On the twenty fifth after a Night of Sorrow and Vexation and never Closing my Eyes i Got up and took my Breakfast and then went and purchased a turn in the next Draft which is to be called out in the Morning

Letters loaned by Valpey family

Affectionate Parents 1814

Charleston S C Feb^r 16

Dear parents I am very Sorry to Imform you that I am Oblidged for to Go on Board of a Privateer I was Dischardged on Monday the 14 Ins^t and Yesterday I Entered on Board of the Schooner Herald of New York of twelve Guns and one Hundred and forty Men Joseph Miller Commander Bound on the Coast of England for a fore Months Cruise I have all My Wa[ges] Exchanged into Gold and put Safe around My Neck and if I Should Lose My Head My Money goes with it ——— williams abbot and Willis Left this port Last Evening for the Northward Expecting for to Reach Boston and with Me there is Gwinn— Lambert and Gray and Bertram of Salem I have a Good Station on Board and I Shall Go on Board this Evening and Sail the first Wind So Give My Love to Brothers and Sisters and Enquiring Frinds

Yours &c

Joseph Valpey Jr.

Halifax Prison August ^{the} 27

1814

Melvill Island

Affectionate Parents

I Embrace this Oppertunity by writing a few Lines to imform you of My safe Arival we was Captured on the 15th by the Frigates Armied & Endymion after being at Sea Six Months from Charleston during the Cruise we Captured ten Sail seven we man'd out and three we Burnt I have been Imformed that there is two Arrived Safe into America but I shall Make My Self Contented until I have the Pleasure of Seeing You and Family Last Monday there was a Number of Hundred American Prisoners Sent to England there is Now five Hundred and fifty Prisoners here and I have not the

Least thoughts of being at Home until the Next Fall our Provisions here is as Good as a Prisoner Can Expect ——— I have Heard of the Death of My Brother Samuel* by William Edwards of Salem but I Cannot Hear from you nor have Not since I Left you I have been Imformed Williams and Abbot did Get Safe home so Remember my Respects to my Brother and Sister and all Enquiring Friends ———
So I Remain yours &c More

Joseph Valpey Jr.

P S Be sure and Write if you have an Oppertunity

---

*Samuel Valpey served on the frigate, Constitution. On her return from the victorious summer voyage of 1812, he was drafted for service on the Great Lakes where he died.

[31]

FROM DEATH⁸ AREST NO AGE IS FREE*

[DRAWING]

Sacred
to
THE
memory
of
WILLIAM PHIPPEN

He sailed from Salem March 13th and whas Drowned the 18th A. D. 1823. from on board of the Schooner Union, James Harvey Master, Bound to the West Indias.

Done by George Valpey Sunday May 2ᵈ 1824.

Sacred
to the Memory of
Josiah Gwinn who Died at
Dartmoor Prison England
on the 22 of Febʳ 1815 A E 22

[DRAWING]†

SACRED
to the Memory of
Daniel Very who died at Dartmoor Prison England
on the 24 of January 1815

also

Mʳ Daniel Archer who died at
Dartmoor Prison England on the 14
of January 1815

---

*Pasted on the first recto following the Journal. The drawing is of a funeral urn bearing the initials, W. P., beside which is a weeping female figure. George Valpey was a brother of Joseph Valpey, Jr

†A crude water color sketch of a hill at the foot of which is a grave with skull and cross-bones.

of Dartmore Prison

1th

of dartmore prison I'll tel all I can
Describe the condition of ten thousand men
there manner of pastime and how they all are
discribe these fine Buildings and how we all fare

2

on top of a mountain those prisons does stand
A place pich^t on purpose for tormenting man
Where Frenchmen and yankey's together must stay
Until the war's o'er or else run away

3

our manner of Living depend's very bad
Not Grub half enough every Countanance sad
Nor clothing sufficient to cover our skin
And no more Indulgence we get from the King

4

Our manner of pastime its hard to Explain
But Keeno and dice is our principal game
While some set at drinking together they sing
Bad luck to the prison short life to the King

6

Now place all together of what I relate
And had I not Reason's for to god dam'n my fate
But I bear it with patience and cheerfully sing
Long life to our President and a curse on the King

The Fruits of Gambling's

1

Come fellow prisoner's one and all
To reason lend an ear
To keep up Gambling as you do
Your ruin'd men its Clear

2

For reason first should Beasly* hear
How we this money use'd
He^d say the prisoner's was to Blame
they that the states abusd.

3

The money that's sent was for intent
To help us in this place
Instead of which you all must see
It clothes you in disgrace

*the Agent for Prisoner's

4

For should you ask for any more
as each man ought to do
Then would your Injured Country say
No money more for you

5

For reason why when i advance
To you this trifling sum
You keep up gambling Night and day
Which hurts you every one

6

Yet a few it help's—a little while
But mark his Latter end
His Bank get's broke, his dunnage sold
This Man's without a Friend

7
Then stealing next is there intent
Which often time's you see
Then be seized up like any dog
And flogged he must be

8
This story's told when he gets home
Unto his Friend's or wife
This man's dispised by them—he Loved
Therefore he cannot value Life

9
To now avoid those Ill's i'v stated
From Gambling now refrain
Then you'll be helped and Respected
Should you ever get home again

The author on Viewing his fellow prisoners hunting for Lice and Fleas Composed the following

1
In Yallow dress from head to foot
Just like a swarm of Bee's
From Morn to Night you'll see a sight
of Hunting lice and flea's

2
They skip and crawl most ravingly
And pass from man to man
If they could speak—you'd hear them say
Now catch me if you can

3
The other Morn as I walked out
To take the pleasant Air
I saw a Louse whose Magnitude
With Horror he made me stare

4
Old Traffalgar he pind him fast
And killed him for the Crime
Saying Yesterday was your's my Louse
But now the day is Mine

Suicide

Last Evening John Taylor the son of Capt John Taylor of New York hung himself in Number five prison ——— *

A Song

From court to clown from beau^x to Clown
I dare say each one know's it
Our Grub's too small for one and all
And our Yankey face's show it.

    Chorus
Yankey dudle dudle due
Yankey dodle dandy,
We^r place'd upon a swindging mount
And to the Moon Quite Handy

    2
We^r plac^d upon a Mountain top
Next Neighbours to the Moon sir
We Yankey tars next to the Stars
Expect to get there soon sir

    3
Then we^d Learn luner's perfect head
And assertain the true distance
Should British tar's come to the stars
We'll give them no Assistance

    4
Should we be ordered down again
And to a Cartel going
Then folk's would stare i do declair
And say the Lad's look's knowing

    5
Then we shall tell them that we do
Because we have lived high sir
Had you been there I do declare
A chance but you would have died

---
*Cf. *The Prisoners' memoirs*, by Charles Andrews, 1852 ed. (pp. 72-73).

6

For cold and hungry—Naked too
Each tar was all but Dying
'till Ruben Beasly 'tother day
He thought he^d stop our Crying

7

But if our Congress hear's the fact
Of our great mighty Income
Then they will stare all with dispair
And say it was a too small sum

8

Then they'll curse Beasly in a Clinch
And call him a dam'n Villen
I'd do so too and so ought you
For it ought to have been one Shilling

9

However lads we'll see it out
Three Coppers come's quite handy O
They'll get a pint of Beer my Boy's
For Yankey dudle dandy O

Where smiling peace and plenty dwell
And health with Jocund glee
No Conjuror one would think could tell
Why war's and strife could be

Valpey

A Song

1

A dew to the shore's of Columbia
Though distant ——— I still you adore
My prospect at present looks gloomy
And I fear i shall see you no more

2
My fortitude its all but Exhausted
I sigh and Lement but's in vain
My Country i fear has forgot me
And i doubt if I see you again

3
Twelve Month's now I'v Languish'd in prison
Each moment seem'd a twelve month for me
Columbia awake from your Slumber's
We prisoner's are awaiting for thee

4
Expecting each day some glad tiding
But nothing alas do we hear
To languish and die in this prison
Is my doom from above i much fear

5
Fond hope's keep's me still in Existence
But misery makes me dispair
Oh Heaven's pray issue an order
And say to the states now tell us prepare

6
Oh Bless^t be that day should it happen
My soul in what raptures would be
I'd fly with the wing's of Impatience
Till Columbia i landed on thee.

[Here is copied "An Oration delivered on the Fourth of July 1814 on Board of the Nassau prison ship by an American Prisoner of War" which has already been printed in *A Journal of a young man of Massachusetts* by Benjamin Waterhouse, 2d ed., 1816 (pp. 121-123). It is followed by a copy of a "Poem wrote by Thomas Sturtevant Junr of the 25 Regim^t of the United States Infantry during his imprisonment at Melville's [Island] Nova Scotia in 1813." This has been printed in *The Diary of Benjamin F. Palmer, privateersman,* published by the Acorn Club, 1914 (pp. 227-239).]

New Year Song
Dartmore Prison January th 1 1815

The new year commences and nature sweet smiling
Salutes the blith nymph and the braw rustic swain
With prospects of pleasure the moments beguiling
And still the bound prisoner must unnoticed Remain
While round the rich Table the wine bumper's flowing
Enliven's each guest with new graces adorning
While hope cheer's the bosom with raptures all glowing
The war broken sailor and soldier must mourn
Behold the gay ball room adorn'd with mock Roses
Where Venus presiding bear's absolute sway
Where love her ten Thousand allurments diffuses
Where hosts of young cupids incessantly play
Where Notes of sweet music hail Cyntha arisen
And Hearts all Enchanted with tenderness burn
Shut out from enjoyments Lock'd up in a prison
The war Broken Sailor and Soldier must mourn
How fortune delusive her favour's disperses
How vain our fond hope's of her Bounty Appear's
While Thousand's enjoy her new sorrow Commence's
And naked and needy we hail the new Year
O soon may sweet peace her mild lucid Blessing
O soon may the morn of Freedom return
Hail Freedom and peace Joy's alone worth possessing
O Come and the Prisoner no longer shall mourn

Love

Dearest Eliza what is Love? a dream
A passion often unrequested
An idle poets lilting theme
A thing with which we are delighted

A Song

Compos'd by Thomas Sturtevant Junr
Whilst a prisoner in Quebec August 1813*

1th

Adieu dear land where first I drew
The sweets of Bliss surrounding
Where neither pain nor Grief I new
But alway's peace Abounding
With eager wish those Groves I Trace.
And bar'd from there Returning
And sigh to meet that Lovely face
For which each hour I'm burning

2th

Green be thy plain's columbia dear
And Green thy Lofty Mountain's
Sweet roses every Valey cheer
Where glow's the purling Fountain's
While worn with Grief my heart endure[s]
Sharp pang's and wild Commotion
And till dispair each hope obscure[s]
As tempests cloud's the Ocean

3th

Dear to my soul are those lov'd form
For which each hour I'm sighing
No healing balm my Bosom cheer's
Or save's my hope from dying
Dear Lydia still my heart is your's
Tho' distance doth devide us
On you dear girl while life endur's
I will doat tho' Ill's betide us
A prisoner poor cut of in fight
Confin'd from all enjoyment
Doom'd through each dismal day and night
And live without employment
On Board a ship Moor'd off Quebec
By Centinals Surrounded
My home My Bed the prison deck
My heart with anguish wounded

---

*Cf. *The Diary of Benjamin F. Palmer, privateersman*, 1914 (pp. 267-268, 266).

5th

But soon I hope for sweet release
In realm's of splendid Glory
In scene's of Love in Bowers of peace
Where glow's the blest aurora
There i shall meet my kindred friends
And gain Immortal Treasure
Where war Terrific never end's
In Interrupted pleasure

A Poem

Composed by Joseph Valpey Junr during his Imprisonment at Dartmoor in 1814

Come young people and now attend
To what i'm going to write
Its to your lives i'd have you amend
And not your Creator for to slight
And yet so long he has spared me
For to live in this vain world
And tossed up both too and fro
And through this life for to be hurld
Its i myself a prisoner Lay
Confin'd in a prison strong
From friends and Relation's far away
I was forced wither right or wrong
And it was there i lay bewailing
On my unhappy state
With many a bitter ailing
Yet no remedy could make
At dark when i to my bed did go
For to pass the tegeous Night
I would lay and think with bitter woe
How i did my Maker slight

As I one Morn was walking
For to take the pleasant air
Two young men i heard a talking
It made me stop and for to stare
They were talking of a Lovly Bloom
Who in salem town did dwell
Who by cold Death was call'd to the Tomb
It appeard to shock them as they it told
I stepped up unto them
For to ask who this might be
They told me it was the lovly Hannah
That good and lovly she
Ah is the lovly Maiden gone
So soon after i left My home
I left her in the bloom of Life
For to struggle through this world of strife
O happy Maid thrice happy be
How soon after we shall follow thee
We no not when nor how soon
We shall be called to the silent Tomb
Fathers Mothers Sisters too
Brothers and Relations has bade us adue
And there they must lay with Closed eyes
Until the Lord bids them arise
Now i hope by this you may warning take
And no more Sabbath day's to Break
That we may all in tune be found
Like David's harp of solemn sound
Now May the Lord some pity take
On us poor prisoner's in this state
And move us to the happy shore
And live in peace forever more
Now i think its time to end my song
.... light is out and darkness comes on
.... that soon some pleasure may find
.... the race of humane kind

Finis

The Old Woman

Returning home the other night later than Usual I found an old woman at a door where she Seemed Unable to gain admittance— Madam said I—May I ask the reason of your Coming home so Late—I have been to take Care of a Sick person but as I have Already been up two nights they are afraid...shall fall asleep and sent me a way — ...have let you sleep in the house where you Was Employd — I feared that I should ... Troublesome, at my age sir we are not ... but in Cases of the Most Urgent Need ... Old Woman had Just Quitted ... You here Yet — Cried he, your ... You again, I beg you will return ... Woman returned, I saw that she...destitute of imformation — She was highly... That the sick person had sent for her again I went with her in order to have a little more talk with ... ——— Women said she to me ——— are Men's Nurses ... They are often praised but never Sufficiently Valued When a Man See's a Woman what ought he t... In her ——— his Nurse ——— his Guardian ——— his Mistress his Wife ——— his Unceasing Friend ——— his Co... ...tenderness but in Woman ——— ... but in old Woman ——— Young ...stantly occupied in taking Care of ... — but as for Me when I am Employd ...the sick I have an Eye to Every thing ... fear that the want of Sleep will weigh My Eyelids down Make Me become pale or Even Indispos'd, A sick person never Constrains him self with an old Woman ——— I felt that this woman knew Exceedingly well The Utility of her age, still the door was Unopend ... I knocked but no Answer was Made — at th... ... that the ... in distress — the being that gave him his first Life — that afforded him his first food — who is the Creator and prompter of every pleasure he Enjoys during his Life — and who's tender attention can alleviate the dreadfull pang's of approaching dissolution — — Young she is beautiful — old she is Good — ...one greatful word overpay's her — Old Women are fitt for a Number of things that Young one's are Incapable of performing — Either from Ignorance or Because they will not take the trouble — I wish that Society knew better how to Value and Re... ... Good old Lady's

American Tar*

Composd in dartmoor Prison England

1th

You son's of Columbia that now ploughs the Ocean
Come listen a while and i'll sing you a Song
Concerning the Eagle the American Standard
And Composed by a Sailor in a prison so Strong

2th

In dartmoor prison you son's of Commotion
[I f]ear we are all doomed to the horror's of war
[Bu]t our prowd Bird the Eagle is sweeping the Ocean
And claiming the rights of American tars

3

[Our] Eagle at home in the forest sat Amusing
With her eyes like the hawk she discovered afar
It was the British proud nation to drive from the Ocean
the Sons of Columbia the American tar

4

so when she took wing on the sea Coast a hovering
her Eyes full of vengence and Bright as the Stars
She said to her heroes Commanding her Navy
Go — defind all the rights of American Tar's

5

On the salt briney ocean our Eagle is a hovering
Directed by Neptune Assisted by Mars
Our Brave Constitution with fix't Ressolution
Commenc'd all the rights of American tars

6

Our banners displayd on the ocean are flying
Decator and Hull wear the Stripes and the Stars
When the Battle of Champlain was won by McDonald
then England acknowledged the American tars

7

our Peacock and wasp are attached to the Eagle
With Death in there Mouths breath Distress afar
While the Reindeer and avon are sent to old davy
Must acknowledg the valour of American tars

---

*Cf. *The Dairy of Benjamin F. Palmer, privateersman*, 1914 (pp. 269-270).

8
but our seamen Empressed in a Prison they are [dying]
Saying beat foe's from our Coast drive your Enemies afar
You ave ever Established for the American tar

9
but our bull dog's are Loose and roaring like Thunder
Destruction and Vengence flies under those stars
So give up those Seamen that you have Impressed
And say you have Injured the American Tars

The Disconsolate Sailor

1
When my Money was all gone that i gaind in the wars
and the world 'gan to frown on my fate
What matter'd my Zeal or my honoured Scar's
when indifference stood at each Gate

2
the face that would smile when my purse was well lind
Shew'd a different Aspect to Me
and when that i could nought but Ingratitude find
I hi'd once again to the Sea

3
I thought it unwise to repine at My Lot
or to bear the Cold looks on the Shore
So I pack'd up the trifling remains I'd got
And a trifling alas was my Store

4
a handkerchief held all the treasures i had
Which over My Shoulder i threw
Away then I trudg'd with a heart rather sad
to Join some Jolly Ship's Crew

5
the Sea was less troubled by far then My Mind
for when the wide Main I Survey'd
I could not helping the world was unkind
And fortune a Slippery Jade

6

And i vowed if once more i could take her in tow
I'd let the ungreatful one see
that the turbulent winds and the billows could show
More kindness than they did to ME

By Joseph Valpey Junr During His Imprisonment At Dartmoor, Devenshire, England March ^{the} 10—1815

1

I tel thee sweet Girl could I time retrieve
and could again begin to Love and Live
to you i would My earlyest off-rings give
I know my Eye's would Lead my heart to you
And I should all my oaths and vows renew
And to be plain I never would be true

2

For by our weak and weary truth i find
Love hates to center in a point assignd
But run's with Joy the Circle of the Mind
Then never let us chain what should be free
But for relief either sex agree
But women loves to Change and so do we

A Song by the Same

1

I've known what 'tis to face a foe
Where death has laid his hundred's Low
What 'tis fatigues to undergo
    that might appall our Nature
Yet never was a truth more clear
that man's in danger — Least in fear
Who's heart can shed a generous tear
    to relieve a fellow prisoner

2
I've seen stout hearts of whom one wave
has in a moment made a Grave
Who's lives not all the World Could save
    then things affect our Nature
But not so much as when the heart
Some ray of Comfort to Impart
Swells up a generous tear to Start
    to relieve a fellow prisoner

A Song

the Author when he was Expecting daly for to get
Released from his Imprisonment Compos'd the following
                                        J Valpey Jr

The heavy hour is almost past
That part my Love and Me
My Longing eyes may hope at Last
There only hope to see

But how my Lydia will you meet
The man you've Lost so long
Will love in all your pulses beat
And tremble on your Tongue

Will you in Every Look declair
Your heart is still the same
And heal each Idle anxious care
Our fears in absence fraim

Thus Lydia thus i paint the scene
When shortly we shall meet
And try what yet remain's between
Of Loit'ring time to Cheat

But if the dream that sooths my mind
Shall false and Groundless prove
If I am doom'd at Length to find
You have forgot to Love

All i of Venus ask is this
No more to Let us Join
But grant me here the flattering Bliss
To live and think you no more mine
Finis

The Sharks of Dartmoor

Compos'd by a American prisoner of War in
Dartmoor Prison England March th 15 — 1815

th1

Come all ye fellow prisoner's attend to what i say
the Presidents Ratification arrived Yesterday
Prepare yourselves for Marching to Prison bid adieu
To shortland and his Turnkey's and all his cursed crew

2

We'll bid adieu to dartmoor there Potatoes Coal and Turf
There barley Bread and Turnips and dam'n Doctors stuff
There codfish and herrin no more of that we'll use
But leave it behind for Doctors clerks Turnkey's & Jews

3

We have done with your Messing out' or will have very soon
The prison then you may inspect three time's in the forenoon
Your Marketing then you may stop your Porter and small Beer
And your Poison Rum and Viteral that has killed hundred's here

4

Grant us but one small favour then before that we do part
Do not discharge the Turnkey's but use them in your cart
The Doctors too you will also keep the prison's for to Clean
And have then all in readiness for Spaniards French or Dean's

5

Your doctors you can well Employ as you shall Quickly find
In washing of the Lousy bed and beding left behind
The turnkey's Louse the Blankets' the hammocks next unsling
The clerks shall mark tham all a new' when turnkey's home do bring

6

Ye cursed tribe of dartmoor attention pray now give
You know when Yankey Tar's are gone you Cannot cannot live
for Murder then you will commit and robberies also
Until like Convict's you are sent to Botany bay must go

7

Make no delay but send us of I tell you for your good
That we may once return again and Bring you back some food
Not you alone but many to keep' you from a Starvation
for Yankey's they have allway's fed your proud Infernal Nation

8

Our President has sent for us' so do not us detain
For fear that he should war declare & Your honour blast again
Do not Blockade the ports of France of Holland or of Spain
For fear the Wasp and Constitution should visit you again

9

I pray you'll give attention and strive to learn my song
as it will be of use to you when Yankey tars are gone
It will remind you of your Living the like you ne'er had before
Nor never will again till we return to Dartmoor

10

No never then shall we return' itts mark now what I say
Until Columbia flag no more shall triumph on the sea's
But until then free Trade' and Sailors righth shall wear
And our Gallant Independence the saucy flag shall Bear

11

I hope that you will attend on some appointed day
And pay respect to Yankey's before we go away
You know it your duty you cannot well deny
So mind and pull your hats off when Yankey's shall pass [by]

12

Fare well you sharks of dartmoor the day at length arrives
Behold the Yankey's marching with tears all in your eyes
Adieu my loving Countrymen that behind the wall's do lay
But your scotch and Irish Doctors no more of us shall slay

13

The happy day will soon arive to sail for Freedoms shore
With six thousand hearty fellow's I think there is no more
The high Lands of Neversink they now appear in sight
The Narrow's next we pass' where we Anchor for all Night

14

Next morning we'll get under way and next our Yards do man
...Cheer those sons of Liberty before that we do land
[Th]en free Trade and Sailors then every Tongue shall cry
[Wh]ile at our foremast head the very flag shall wear

(Finis)

Sacred to the Memory of Josiah Gwinn

Go spotless honour and unsullied Truth
Go smilling Inocence and Blooming youth
Go Male sweetness Join'd in Manly sence
Go winning wit that never gave offence
Go soft humanity that Blest the poor
Go saint eye'd patience from afflicktions door
Go Modesty which never gave a frown
Go Virtue and receive thy heavenly Crown
Not from a stranger came this heart felt verse
Thy Friend inscribes thy Tomb Where tears
         Bedewd thy hearse

                    by Joseph Valpey Ju[r]

British Massacree

the following is a list of the Men who were so Inhumanly Murdered on the ever to be Remembered th6 day of April 1815

KILLED

Prisons
Nº 1   John Mann

Nº 4   John Haywood
"   Thomas Jackson

Nº 5   John Washington
"   William Leverige
"   Joseph Johnson
"   George Cambell

WOUNDED

Nº 1   John Gray left arm amputated
"   John Ogleby in the left hip
"   Stephen Phillips Left thy and Belly

Nº 3   Edward Gardner in the wrist
"   James Bell in the wrist and thy
"   Phillip Ford in the side Brest and arm
"   James Trumbull left arm Amputated
"   Edward Whittlebank in the Back
"   William Blake several places in the Body
"   Caleb Codders two places in the leg
"   Thomas Smith left leg amputated

Nº 4   John Robberts in the Thigh
"   Peter Wilson in the hand
"   James Isreal in the thigh
"   Jacob Davis in the thigh
"   William Penn in the Belly
"   Robert Little left thigh amputated
"   Joseph Busah in the thigh
"   Robbert Willet left thigh amputated

*Cf. *The Prisoners' memoirs*, by Charles Andrews for "a correct list of killed and wounded on the 6th of April, 1815...contains a true statement of their condition at 12 o'clock on the 8th day of the same month," 1852 ed. (pp. 100-108); also the official report of the American agent, R. G. Beasley, in *American state papers* [Gales and Seaton ed.] *Foreign relations*, v. 4, 1834 (pp. 52-54).

N° 5 Thomas Finley in the thigh
" William Appleby in the arm
" John Leach in the thigh
" Andrew Garrison Head and hand
" John Giar left leg amputated
" William Lane in the Eye
" Pain Penny in the Shoulder

N° 7 James Willis in the arm and two places in the Body
" Henry Mountcalm in the Knee
" Frederic Howard in the leg
" Edward Lincoln in the thigh
" Francis Mitchel in the arm
" Michal Cannors in the arm

a Number more was slightly wounded and Several Missing.

[52]

A List of the Names of the American prisoners who Died in the hospital dartmoor England*

Name	Date			Vessels' Names	Place of Residence
A					
Adigo henry	Dec.	23,	1813	U. S. Brig. Argus	Howisburg
Alamanza Amos	Sep.	24,	1814	President	Carthagina
Adams Jno	Nov r.	6,	"	Grey hound	Washington N C
Allen Asy	"	14,	"	Herald	New Bedford
Allen John	"	21,	"	Herald	New York
Andrews Josiah	"	22	"	David Porter	Ipswich Mass
Adams John	Dec r. th 3		"	do	Unknown
Anderson Alexan d	"	29	"	Criterion	New York
[torn]	Feb. th 5		1815	Herald	Unknown
				[Grand] Turk	Salem portsmouth
Appleton Daniel	Jan.	4	1815	Frolick	Ipswich Mass
Amos Peter	Feb.	18	"	Napolean	Vinyard
B					
Barron Thomas	Nov.	3	1813	Argus	Virginia
Blanchard Nich a.	May th 5		"	Armied	Unknown
Bryant Louis	Nov b.	3	1814	Hawk	North Caroline
Bray Ezikiah	"	20	"	Ida	Boston
Butman John	"	23	"	died suddenly in the prisen	
Benn William	"	27	"	Indipendence	Virginia
Berry Peter	"	28	"	Chapine [?]	Baltimore
Burley Henry	Dec r	2	"	Ampressive [?]	New York
Baldwinn Jno	-	5	"	Fox	Boston
Barrett Jason	-	8	"	Buisy	pensylvania
Barber henry	-	25	"	Grey Hound	Virginia
Booth James	-	29	"	Victory	New Hamphery
[torn] bb Benjamin	Jan	29	1815	———	New York
Blasdell Wm	Jan	10	"	Impressed	portsmouth N h
Beak Wm	-	19	"	taken at fort Erie	do
Brady Wm	"	20	"	Harlequin	Lee N H
Berry George	Feb	14	"	Piker	Baltimore
Brown Charles	"	17	"	Paul Jones	unknown
Bayley Moses	"	17	"	Scorpion	Philadelphia
Butter John	"	23	"	Simerma	Deleware
Blew John	Jan	1	1813	Frolick	providence
Blazed Phillip	"	10	"	———	New hamps[hire]
C					
Cornish Charles	"	10	1813	Chesapeak	Baltimore
Cole James	Apr	20	"	Unknown	Wiscasset
Cook Benj	"	6	"	Chesapeak	Baltimore
Collins Jno	Oct	7	"	Mamouth	unknown
Carney Jno	"	16	1813	Flash	Virginia
Chandler simon	"	25	"	Essex	Duxbury
Coleman Wm	Nov	5	1814	Hawk	N. Carolina

---

*Cf. The *Prisoners' memoirs*, by Charles Andrews for similar lists: "of the prisoners who died at Dartmoor from April 1813 until the 18th February, 1815; copied from the reports of the Doctor," (pp. 144-149) and "a correct list of names of prisoners who died at Dartmoor prison, from February 18, 1815, until April 20, 1815," (pp. 149-151).

[53]

Name	Date			Vessel's Name	Place of Residence
Cooper Thos.	"	8	"	Flora	Rhode Island
Cool John	"	26		Adeline	Baltimore
Coffee John	Dec	4	"	———	Long Island
Campeachy C	Jan	19	"	President	Carthagina
Clark simon	"	24	"	Snap Dragon	New England
Clarke Wm	Jul	10	1813	Unknown	
Carter Wm	Oct	5	1814	Zephyr	New York

D

Dalton Wm	May	10	"	Argus	Georgia
Donouer Wm	Nov	12	1813	Syren	Massachusetts
Denham Silus	Nov	14	1814	Ida	Boston
Daltram [?] Amo	"	18	"	Ida	New Bedford
Diamond Wm	Jan	23	1815	Mary	Rhode Island
Dagget Thomas	Mar	14	1814	Argus	Mass

E

Edsad Wm	Jan	27	"	Hepsa	New Jersey
Earens Edward	"	6	1815	North star	———

F

Freely Henry		20	1814	Impressed	Pensylvania
Fullford Ibs^r	"	27	1814	Snap Dragon	N. Carolina
Furnal Wm	"	23	"	Harper	portsmouth
Fowler Jeshua	Dec	30	"	Impressed	Boston

G

Goselin Thos	Apr	29	"	Augustine	Martinique
Gibson Wm	Oct	22	"	Rattle Snake	New York
Gardner Francis	Nov	4		Rambler	Rhode Isla[nd]
Gailon Jno	Dec	3		America	N. Carolina
Gudman Franc	Feby	17	1815	Bunkerhill	Portsmouth
Gwinn Josiah	"	22	"	Herald	Salem
Greeves Thos	"	27	"	Portershan [?]	Boston

H

Hughes Richa	"	5	1814	Amiable	New York
Harris simen	March	5	1814	Madalem [?]	New York
Henry Jason	July	d3	"	Argus killed fighting	N York
Heart Jos	"	8	"	Courier	New York
Herman Isaac	Nov	9	"	Elbridge Gerry	Portland
Hetrope Jas	"	4	"	Mary	Cambridge
Harris Wm		24		———	Portsmouth N H
Hyder Dempsey	Dec	24	"	Paul Jones	N Carolina
Hendy Jacob	Feb	5	"	Impressed	Milford Cont
Hartford Elias	Jan	6	1815	Soldier	———
Hadison silas	Dec	4	1814	Hawk	N. Carolina
Holden Francis	Feb	24	"	Rattle snake	Virginia

J

Jones Thomas	Jun	6	1813	Impressed	———
Joseph Peter	Feb	26	1815	President	Martinico
Jackson Thomas	June	5	1813	Hybias	New York
Johnson Elisha	Nov^r	2	"	William	Charleston
Joseph Emanuel	"	25	1814	Impressed	Oporto [?]

[54]

Name	Date			Vessel's Name	Place of Residence
Johnson Jno	Feb	1	1814	Criterion	New York
Jones John	"	8	1815	President	St Thomas
Jenkins Edward	"	21	"	Tom	Cambridge
Jones Jacob	"	23	"	Impressed	Maryland
Jaires Thomas	Jan	24	1814	Industry	Marblehead
Jenkins John	Feb	24	"	Hawke	Gay head
K					
King Uriah	"	3	"	Dominica	Scituate mass
Knapp James	"	27	1815	President	———
L					
Lester Jason	Jan	1	1813	Mars	Baltimore
Lewis Jno	Aug	5	"	Yankey	Rhode Island
Larkin Lewis	Sep	30	"	Rolla	Darham N H
Lovely Pr	Nov	1	1814	Hawk	Washington N C
Lovel Joseph	"	3	"	President	Martinico
Lamb Anthony	"	22	"	Grand Turk	Connecticut
Larkin Amos	Jan	27	1814	Empressed	Beverly Mass
Lufkey Jas	Feb	4	"	Enterprize	Marble head
Lee Richard	Dec	30		Alevant	Portland
Leopatch Jno	Feb	9		ann	Mass
M					
Moor henry	Jan	14	1814	Mermaid	New York
Montgomery Jno	Feb	24	1813	———	New York
Martin Daniel	Sep	22	"	Paul Jones	New Orleans
Medoza Charles	Oct	th 27	1814	President	Cathergina
Merry Jno	Nov	18	"	Rattle snake	Baltimore
Mesler Richard	Nov	20	"	Snap Dragon	Unknown
Martial Saul	"	20	1814	Alexander	Mass
Mitchel Jno	Jany	12	1815	Charlotte	———
Mudge Joseph	Dec	30	1814	Unknown	
Morrison Wm	"	14	"	Impressed	Baltimore
Martin Jno	"	17	"	President	Cathergena
Menter Charles	Feb	27	"	Merchant	Portugal
Miller Edward	"	23	1815	Mamouth	New York
Marchens Jesse	"	3	"	McDonough	Kenebunk
N					
Norton Edward	Novr	29	1814	Frolick	weymouth
Nash Daniel	Feb	14	"	———	
P					
Pierce Saml	Mar	12		Dart	Rhode Island
Pinkham Ephra	Sept	25	1814	Mamouth	Wiscassett
Potters Jno	Oct	5	"	Impressed	Philidelphia
Potters G I	"	7	"	Enterprize	Salem
Perkins Jas	Nov	3	"	Syren	Pitsfield
Palmer Jno	"	17	"	Frolick	Portsmouth
Pollard George	"	23	"	Ida	Salem
Paroga Jos	"	24	"	Ida	Boston
Parker Wm	"	28	"	Independence	Virginia
Peters Aaron	Jan	30	"	Joel Barlow	Thomas town
Porter Charles	"	14	"	———	
Peterson Saml	Dec	9	"	Nonsuch	philidelphia

[55]

Name	Date			Vessel's Name	Place of Residence
R					
Renew Benja	Nov	16	"	Fox	Guadaloupe
Rodgers Luke	"	12	"	Fairy	N Carolina
Reed David	Nov	14	1814	America	towns end
Robertson frank	Feb	7	"	Chesapeak	Spain
Rice Thomas	"	15	"	Salvador	Suffolk
Robertson Saml	"	15	1815	———	Boston
S					
Saunders Wm	Jan	16	"	Mars	Baltimore
Shaw Wm	Oct	17	1814	Argus	Philidelphia
Saul frances	"	20	"	Mercury	Wiscasset
Sawyer Jed	"	25	"	Impressed	Providence
Studdy Richa	Nov	3	"	Amelia	Virginia
Simpson Isaac	Dec	20	"	Invincible	New York
Stow Lewis	"	21	"	Tickler	New York
Smart Wm	"	5	"	Gothland	Virginia
Sew Jacob	"	7	"	Volunteer	New York
Steel [?] John	"	15	1814	William	Ireland
Sheldon Henry	Jan	24	"	———	
Scudding Sa. [?]	"	19	"	Siro	portland
Strout Jno	"	20	"	Harlequin	Kenebunk
Stow Jno	Jan	5	1815	E———	
Sinamon Dan	"	23	"	Enterprize	Salem
Smith Nichol	Dec	8	1814	Herald	Richmond Va
Sutton Martin	Feb	22	1815	Lyon	New Bedford
Simmon Eben^r	Jan	20	"	———	———Bar
T					
Terry Wm	Feb	15	1813	Viper	Unknown
Tobby Elijah	Mar	9	1814	Yankey	New York
Thomas Uriah	Jul	23		Paul Jones	Connecticut
Timmon M.:	Feb	26	1813	Tom	New York
Tomas John	Oct	25	1813	Lion	
Tuttle Francis	Nov	24	1814	E Gerry	N York
Tailor J B	Dec	2	"	hung himself in No. 5 prison) N York	
Tophouse Sam	Feb	13	1813	Soldier	
Thomas Henry	"	24	1815	Clarence	Sloughton
Tomkins K	Nov	13	1814	Unknown	
V					
Vaughn K	Aug	31	"	———	Long Island
Very Daniel	Jan	24	1815	Frolick	Salem
Virgis James	"	8	"	Growler	Marblehead
W					
Williams Tho	March	20	1813	Maria	Georgetown
Williams Jas	Oct	27	1814	Impressed	Gay head
Williams Jas	Feb	1	1815	Carolina	———
Whithan Jno	Jan	14	"	Harlequin	Portsmouth
Wert George	"	28	1815	Harlequin	portsmouth
Y					
Young Wm	"	21	"	Levant	

from the 1 of March 1815 to the first of April following died in the hospital with the Small pox about seventy Americans prisoner of war whose Names is not here Inserted

The
Description of Dartmoor Prison Devonshire
and the
British Massacre on the sixth of April A.D. 1815
by a
Prisoner of War.

DARTMOOR DEPOT is situated in the county of Devonshire* and lies about 15 miles N E of plymouth and 26 miles W N W of exeter the capital town, its appearance and Situation is most unpleasant and disagreeable imaginable, the country around as far as the eye extends is one uneven barren and dreary waste, not a tree Shrub or scarce a plant is seen for many miles around, here and there appears a miserable thatched Cottage whose outward appearance bespeaks the misery and poverty within, here no cheering prospect greets the prisoners eye, bountiful nature here denies all her sweets and seems to simpathize with the unhappy Prisoner the loss of every joy that renders life worth preserving, the climate here is rather unhealthy, the prisoners here are almost allways afflicted with colds and severe pains during 9 months in the year, owing most probably to its height, it being upwards of 1700 feet above the surface of the sea, this Depot consists of 7 Prisons each calculated to contain from 11 to 1,500 men who are under the care of an agent, appointed by and under the controle of the transport board, here are stationed as gaurds upwards of 2000 well disaplined militia & 2 companies of royal Artilary, the Prisons are all strong built of stone and are surrounded with 2 circular walls, the outward wall measures one mile in circumferance and on the inner wall is a milatary walk for Centinels, within this wall distance about 20 feet are, Iron pallisadees about 10 feet high, adjoining the outward wall are gaurd houses placed N. E. and South there are 3 sepperate gards which communicates with each other through the passage of about 150 feet long & 20 broad gaurded on each side by Iron bars, over which and fronting Nº 4 is a milatary walk for centinals, oposite the passage is the market square in passing into either yard you pass through 2 Iron gates so that all communication may be stopped at pleasure, which is often done to annoy and vex the Prisoners, in the first yard there contains three prisons Nº 1. 2. 3 Nº 1 & 3 are only occupied by the American Prisoners, and Nº 2 stands empty, in the other yard Nº 5 & 7 also are occupied, and Nº 6 stands empty, and Nº 4 for the blacks, the inside of the prisons presents a melancholy and disagreeable aspect and one would imagine they were calculated for cattle rather then the human species, North of no. 1 between the inner wall and Iron railing, stands the condemned Prison, this is a

---

*This account of the Dartmoor massacre, copied by another hand at the close of Joseph Valpey's *Journal*, was evidently used by Edgar S. Maclay in his *History of American privateers*, (1899 ed., p. 367). It has not been found printed in any of the books on this subject which are available for consultation.

place of punishment for various offencies commited by individuals, four persons having been condemned by the government to suffer imprisonment during the war, for attempting to blow a Prize up, this Prison is calculated to contain 60 persons who are allowed a blanket & straw instead of their ordinary bedding, their daily allowance is considerably reduced, a small apperture near the roof admits the light fronting N° 1 yard is a wall seperating it from the Hospital, and fronting the other yard is another wall seperating it from the inner barracks, the market which fronts the passage leading from one prison to the other, is nearly square, and will contain nearly 5000 persons, and is allowed to be opened every day except Sundays at eleven oclock and closed at one, and is productive of no small profits to the country people, at the uper part of the square, are two stone houses, one for Kings and the other for Prisoners stores, the other buildings attatched to this depot are houses for turnkeys and clarks, one for the agent and one for the Doctor; to enter either of the Prisons yards from without, you must pass through 5 gates, fronting the outer gate is a reservoir of water, which is brought the Distance of 6 miles by means of a canal which supplies the differant yards with water; the Hospital is under the superintendance of a Physician who has 2 assistant Doctors, George Magrath the present superintendant, is a gentleman of Eminance and skill in his profession, and will ever be remembered by the American Prisoners. with esteem and respect, the sick have uniformly received from him every attention that delicacy and humanity could dictate, at this time there are 5600 prisoners in this depot, nearly one half of whom are men who have been imprest in his majesties service prior to the war, many hardships have been suffered by the Prisoners more especially in the year 1813 which was exceeding cold and severe, although excessively cold and many of the Prisoners almost naked, no fire was allowed, nor cloathing served to proect their shivering limbs and half famished bodies from the inclemency of the weather, it must be observed that the prisoners at that time received no assistance from their Government and many of them had been rob'd or plundered of their cloathing whereby by the time winter commenced were little short of nakedness —— in april following they received from their inexorable agent M^r. Beasly a suit of cloathing and 2½ p^r. Day, which sum tho' small was a great relief, the prisoners on many occasions have received very injurious and harsh treatment from the Governor of the Depot, having allways endeavored to curtail them of the smallest liberty or indulgence, the recent Massacre which took place by his order ought forever to stamp the name of Thomas George Shortland with cowardice, Barbarity Infamy & disgrace, his name will never be mentioned by a single American Prisoner but with sentiments of detestation horror and contempt ———

On the 6th day of April 1815 as a small party of prisoners were amusing themselves at a game of ball, some one of the number striking it with too much violence it went over the wall fronting the prison the Centinals on the opposite side of the same were requested to heave the ball back, but refused, on which the party threataned to brake through and regain the ball and immediatly put their threats in execution, a hole was made in the wall sufficiently large enough for a man to pass through, but no one attemped it, soon after the alarm bell rung and the milatary beat to arms the prisoners surprised at the alarm run into the Passage opposite the market, when appeared Captain Shortland at the head of about 500 of the Malitia, the front rank of whom were ordered to fire, and soon after the rear done the same, with considerable execution and persued the Prisoners to the yards, the Scenes of barbarity and horror which were witness'd on this Day are indiscribable, 9 were killed and 38 were wounded, six of whom lost their legs and arms, and many others severely wounded; a man by name John Washington being wounded and overtaken by the milatary begged for his life but those Ruffians deaf to the voice of pity, deliberatly pointed their muskets within six inches of his head and blew his brains out, a young lad aged fourteen was run through the body by an officer of the milatary, many other instances of the most savage barbarity took place on this fatal day scarce a single person that was thus persecuted knew the cause thereof: ——— Captain Shortland endeavours to justify his conduct by saying the prisoners were attempting to break out so far from that being the case the prisoners were in momentary expectation of being drafted on board Cartels, and had the prison gates been thrown open, scarce a single person of five thousand would have left the Prison; it is a notorious fact that Capt. Shortland has long sought a plausible pretext to glut his revenge and hatred against men whose principles and manners are so incongruous with those of his countrymen in general

---

The 6th of April will long be remembered with emotions of horror and grief by every American Prisoner, with horror at the savage furosity of the milatary headed by Capt. Shortland; with grief at the untimely Death of their unprotected and defenceles Brethren; ———— w[h]ere ye britons on that day was your boasted valour,,, ———— was it displayed in your wanton attack on a few defenceless men;—w[h]ere was your vaunted generosity and clemency was it in opening the Prison doors and discharging Vollies of musketry at the prisoners within, where was the amity and Friendship so lately pledged by your government: ———— was it shewn in wantonly murdering those brave and unfortunate men who had been struggling for their rights: ———— where sleeps the sword of justice, that should revenge our wrongs: ———— behold the assasin beneath the protection of despot Tyrants, securely tryumph and bid defiance to Justice; Oh Shame where is thy blush; oh cowardice where is thy confusion ———— but know ye bloody butchers of our slaughtered countrymen that millions of free born sons of liberty, shall ere long revenge their murdered Brethren, Ere long shall the avenging Sword of justice leap from its scabbard and bid defiance to tyranny and oppression

Farewell ye unfortunate friends who fell untimely victims of barbarity, no more shall you be partakers of our joy, or the pleasing companions of our social hours, no more shall the musick of festivity or the welcome embrace of those you held most dear, dilate your hearts with joy, or attune your souls to harmony and love, farewell ye murdered brethren; the innocent victims of inhuman assasins, Peace in vain extended her cheering olive, in vain did justice Humanity or mercy plead in your behalf. ———— in vain did you beg for a moment to prepare yourselves for eternity Ye tender and affectionate Parents who are now anticipating the happy return of your affectionate children how will the cup of anticipated bliss be dashed to the ground when you receive the fatal news of their untimely Deaths; no more shall the musick of their voices sound delightful to your ears; no more shall their affectionate regards reward the parental care of their early youth; well may ye curse the distroyers of your happiness, the butchers of your sons

Ye disconsalate and unprotected widows who with fond Solicitude are awaiting to welcome and press to your affectionate hearts the partners of your bosoms; how will your hearts throb with anguish and your bosoms fill with woe when the tale of horror is repeated and their loss confirmed

Behold the Widows arms extended to embrace the dear pledges of their mutual loves while they in lisping accents in vain repeat the name of Father, ye helpless orphens babes, no more shall ye receive the tender caresses of your affectionate father, no more shall ye be dandled on the Knee or receive from his glowing lips the kisses of Paternal affection, Ye sons of Columbia the Blood of your slaughtered countrymen Cries to you from the ground avenge our Deaths ⸺

remember the 6th of April AD 1815

Letters

from Joseph Valpey Junr. to His Friends
in the Hospital

Dartmoor

March th1 1815

[64]

from J Valpey Jr to Josiah G[winn]

February th6 1815

Dear Friend

having Not heard from you Since you went into the Hospital it makes me feel Very desirous to hear from you I would be much Obliedged to you if you would Send me a few Lines And Direct it to the N°. 7 Prison Mess N°. 129

Yours &c   Joseph Valpey Jun.

from Josiah [Gwinn]
to Joseph Valpey Jr

February th7 1815

Dear Friend

I send you a few Lines to Imform you that I am as well as can be Expected with the Small Pox I wish that you would take care of my Clothes that [you] have in your Possesion So I Remain your Sincere Friend till Death &c

Josiah Gwinn

Hospital
    Ward N°. 1

[fr]om Joseph Valpey Jr
to Edward A Porter

Feby. th10 1815

Esteemed Friend

According to promise I Send you a few Line's and as not having heard from you since you Left us I wish that you would Enquire after Josiah Gwinn and write to me as soon as you can make it Convinent and by so doing you Will Obliedge your's &c

Joseph Valpey Junr

[from] Edward A Porter
[to Jo]seph Valpey Jun[r]

N° 5 Ward Feb[y] [th]11 1815

Dear Friend

I Improve the Present opportunity to Inform you that I have made perticular Enq[uiry], After Mr. Gwinn—I am Imformed that his Life is dispaired off I however hope that he may get over it I am In hopes to be out in t[he] Course of a week—Sir i wish for a little Cash [if it?] were possible to procure it—

yours E A Porter

Bibliography

[Abbatt, William.] Dartmoor Prison and the church memorial. (Magazine of history, with notes and queries, July, 1910. v. 12, p. 66-69, front.)

[Andrews, Charles.] The prisoners' memoirs. N. Y., 1815.

—— —— N. Y., 1852.

Catel, L. La prison de Dartmoor. Paris, 1847.

Clay, Henry. [Letter to James A. Bayard, London, April 28, 1815. Dartmoor massacre and transportation of prisoners to America.] (American historical association. Annual report, 1913. v. 2, p. 380-382.)

Cobb, J. A. A younker's first cruise. 1841.

Dartmoor Prison as it was and as it is. (Fraser's magazine, November, 1853. v. 48, p. 577-587.)
Reprinted in Eclectic magazine, January, 1854. v. 31, p. 123-131, and in Littell's Living age, December 10, 1853. v. 39, p. 671-678.

Hawthorne, Nathaniel, *ed.* Papers of an old Dartmoor prisoner. (*In* United States magazine and Democratic review, 1846. New series. v. 18-19.)

McNeel, John Greenville. American prisoners at Dartmoor. (Harper's monthly magazine, September, 1904. v. 109, p. 548-555.)

[Palmer, Benjamin Franklin.] The diary of Benjamin F. Palmer, privateersman. N. Y., 1914. (Acorn club, Publication 11.)

Pierce, Edward L. Communication:—The American prisoners at Dartmoor. (Massachusetts historical society. Proceedings, 2d series, 1896. v. 10, p. 116-117.)
—— [Memoranda about Dartmoor Prison communicated by Justin Winsor.] (Massachusetts historical society. Proceedings, 2d series, 1892. v. 7, p. 17-18.)
Reminiscences of a Dartmoor prisoner. (*In* Knickerbocker magazine. 1844. v. 23-24.)
Steele, J. Aulay. America on Dartmoor. (Chambers's journal, June 1, 1918. [v. 95], 7th series, v. 8, p. 424-427.)
Thomson, Basil. The story of Dartmoor Prison. London, 1907.
U. S. *33d Congress, 1st session. House.* Compensation and bounty land to certain American seamen . . . Report . . . Committee on invalid pensions to which were referred the petitions and papers of sundry citizens of Maine, Massachusetts and New York, prisoners in Dartmoor and other British prisons during the war of 1812. (Report, no. 344.)
U. S. *President, 1809-1817 (Madison).* Message . . . transmitting a report of the Secretary of state . . . in obedience to a resolution of the House of representatives of the 4th inst., in relation to the transactions at Dartmoor Prison in the month of April last, so far as the American prisoners of war, there confined, were affected by such transactions. January 31, 1816 . . . Washington, 1816. ([State papers] 36.)
Also in American state papers, [Gales & Seaton ed.] Foreign relations, v. 4, 1834, p. 19-56, under caption, "Great Britain—Massacre at Dartmoor Prison." (14th Congress, 1st session, no. 281.)
—— Message . . . transmitting a report of the Secretary of state in obedience to a resolution of the House of representatives of the 28th of February last, on the number of impressed American seamen confined in Dartmoor Prison; the number surrendered, given up, or taken on board British vessels captured during the late war; together with their places of residence. April 29, 1816 . . . Washington, 1816.
[Waterhouse, Benjamin.] A journal of a young man of Massachusetts, late a surgeon on board an American privateer. Boston, 1816.
—— ——, 2d ed., Boston, 1816.

Fiction

Phillpotts, Eden. The American prisoner, a romance of the west country. N. Y., 1904.
Reynolds, Joseph. Peter Gott, the Cape Ann fisherman. Boston, 1856.

Poetry

Carrington, N. T. Dartmoor: a descriptive poem. 2d ed. London, 1826.
W., I. H. The Dartmoor massacre. 1815 [Reprint, N. Y., 1911]. (Magazine of history, with notes and queries. Extra no. 15 [pt. 2].)

Persons and Vessels Mentioned

Abbot, ——, 29, 30.
Abbot, S., 1, 3.
Abbot, William, 27.
Abbott, W., 14.
Adams, John, 52.
Adams, Robert, 20.
Adeline, 52.
Adigo, Henry, 52.
Akbar (*frigate*), 12.
Alamanza, Amos, 52.
Alevant, 54.
Alexander, 54.
Allen, Asy, 52.
Allen, Henry, 26.
Allen, John, 52.
America (*ship*), vi, 53, 54.
Amiable, 53.
Amos, Peter, 52.
Anderson, Alexander, 52.
Andrews, Josiah, 52.
Ann, 54.
Appleby, William, 51.
Appleton, Daniel, 18, 52.
Archer, Daniel, 18, 31.
Archer, Samuel, 15, 18, 20.
Argus (*brig*), 52, 53, 55.
Armied, [*Armede, Armide*] (*frigate*), 11, 29, 52.
Ashton, William, 14, 15, 16, 18, 19, 20, 22, 23, 25, 26, 27.
Atwill, Mehitable (Valpey), v.
Augustine, 53.
Avon (*brig*), 43.

Baldwinn, John, 52.
Barber, Henry, 52.
Barlow, Joel, see Joel Barlow.
Barrett, Jason, 52.
Barron, Thomas, 52.
Bayley, Moses, 52.
Beak, William, 52.
Beasley, Reuben G., 25, 33, 36, 60.
Beckford, John, 14, 16, 17.
Bell, James, 50.
Benn, William, 52.
Bentley, William, v.
Berry, George, 52.
Berry, Peter, 52.
Bertram, ——, 29.

Blake, William, 50.
Blanchard, Nich[a], 52.
Blasdell, William, 52.
Blazed, Phillip, 52.
Blew, John, 52.
Blind George, *the crier*, 18.
Boden, William, 17.
Bonaparte, [Napoleon], vi, 25.
Booth, James, 52.
Brady, William, 52.
Bray, Ezikiah [!], 52.
Brown, Charles, 52.
Brutus, 20.
Bryant, Louis, 52.
Buisy, 52.
Bunker Hill, 53.
Burley, Henry, 52.
Burton, Clarence Monroe, v.
Busah, Joseph, 50.
Butman, John, 52.
Butman, Nehemiah, 15.
Butter, John, 52.

Cambell, George, 50.
Campeachy, C., 53.
Cannors, Michal, 51.
Carney, John, 52.
Carolina (*schooner*), 55.
Carter, William, 53.
Catharine, see *Little Catharine*.
Chadwick, John, 16.
Chandler, Simon, 52.
Chapine [?], 52.
Charlotte (*brig*), 54.
Chesapeake (*frigate*), 52, 55.
Clarence, 55.
Clark, Simon, 53.
Clarke, William, 53.
Clemons, Gilbert, vi.
Codders, Caleb, 50.
Coffee, John, 52.
Cole, James, 52.
Coleman, William, 52.
Collins, John, 52.
Constitution (*frigate*), 30, 43, 48.
Cook, Benjamin, 52.
Cook, Samuel, 11, 25, 26, 27.
Cool, John, 52.
Cooper, Thomas, 52.

Cornish, Charles, 52.
Courier, 53.
Criterion, 52, 53.
Crowninshield, Bowdoin B., v.

Dagget, Thomas, 53.
Dalton, William, 53.
Daltram [?], Amo, 53.
Dart, 54.
David Porter, 52.
Davis, Jacob, 50.
Decator [Decatur, Stephen], 43.
Denham, Silus [!], 53.
Diamond, William, 53.
Dominica (schooner), 54.
Donouer, William, 53.
Dotterel (brig), 4.

Earens, Edward, 53.
Edsad, William, 53.
Edwards, W., 11.
Elbridge Gerry, 53, 55.
Endymon [Endymion] (frigate), 11, 29.
Enterprize, 54, 55.
Essex (frigate), 52.
Eulin, ——, 17, 22, 26.

Fairy, 54.
Favourite (sloop), 23, 24.
Felt, ——, 14, 15.
Felt, George, 26, 27.
Felt, William, 16.
Finley, Thomas, 51.
Fisher, John, 14.
Flash, 52.
Flora, 52.
Ford, Phillip, 50.
Fowler, Jeshua, 53.
Fox, 52, 54.
Freeland, Frances, see Sir Frances Freeland (*packet*).
Freely, Henry, 53.
Frolick [Frolic], 52, 54, 55.
Fullford, Ibs^r, 53.
Furnal, William, 53.

Gailon, John, 53.
Gale, Edward, 15, 16.
Gardner, Edward, 50.
Gardner, Francis, 53.
Garret, William, 14.
Garrison, Andrew, 51.
General Putnam, 17.

George, *see* Blind George, *the crier*.
Gerry, Elbridge, *see* Elbridge Gerry.
Giar, John, 51.
Gibson, William, 53.
Glover, John H., 1.
Goselin, Thomas, 53.
Gothland, 55.
Gotier, C., 26.
Grand Turk, 52, 54.
Gray, John, 50.
Gray, William, 11, 20, 21, 22, 23, 26, 2 29.
Green, Charles, 15.
Green, Samuel, 15, 17, 25, 28.
Greeves, Thomas, 53.
Greyhound, 52.
Growler, 55.
Gudman, Franc, 53.
Gwinn, ——, *uncle of John Mack*, 23.
Gwinn, Josiah, 11, 14, 15, 19, 20, 21, 2 29, 31, 49, 53, 64, 65.

Hadison, Silas, 53.
Harlequin, 52, 55.
Harper, 53.
Harriot (brig), 5.
Harris, Simen [!], 53.
Harris, William, 53.
Harrison, James, 16, 20.
Hartford, Elias, 53.
Hawk (schooner), 52, 53, 54.
Haywood, John, 50.
Heart, Joseph, 53.
Hendy, Jacob, 53.
Henry, Jason, 53.
Hepsa, 53.
Herald (schooner), vi, 3, 4, 11, 26, 29. 52, 53, 55.
Herman, Isaac, 53.
Hetrope, James, 53.
Holden, Francis, 53.
Hope (ship), vi.
Howard, Frederic, 51.
Hughes, Richard, 53.
Hull, [Isaac], 43.
Hybias, 53.
Hyder, Dempsey, 53.

Ida (brig), 11, 52, 53, 54.
Independence, 52, 54.
Industry, 54.
Ingersoll, John, 15, 26.
Invincible, 55.

nvincible Napoleon (corvette), 11, 52.
.real, James, 50.

.ckson, Thomas, 50, 53.
.ires, Thomas, 54.
.nkins, Edward, 53.
.nkins, John, 54.
.el Barlow, 54.
.hn (schooner), 9.
.hnson, Elisha, 53.
.hnson, John, 53.
.hnson, Joseph, 50.
.nes, ——, *Rev.*, 23.
.nes, Jacob, 54.
.nes, John, 53.
.nes, Paul, see Paul Jones (schooner).
.nes, Thomas, 53.
.seph, Emanuel, 53.
.seph, Peter, 53.

.ing, Uriah, 54.
.napp, James, 54.
.nowlton, Enos, 11.

.amb, Anthony, 54.
.ambert, Samuel, 11, 12, 14, 15, 29.
.ane, William, 51.
.arkin, Amos, 54.
.arkin, Lewis, 54.
.each, John, 51.
.ee, Richard, 54.
.eopatch, John, 54.
.ester, Jason, 54.
.evant, 55.
.everige, William, 50.
.ewis, John, 54.
.incoln, Edward, 51.
.ion (sloop), 55; see also Lyon.
.ittle, Robert, 50.
.ittle Catharine (packet), 7, 8.
.ouis [XVIII], king of France, 25.
.ovel, Joseph, 54.
.ovely, Pr., 54.
.ufkey, James, 54.
.yon, 55; see also Lion (sloop).

lcDonald [Macdonough, Thomas], 43.
lcDonough (brig), 54.
lack, John, 23.
ladalem [?], 53.
lagrath, George, 59.
lajestic (razee), 11.
lamouth [Mammoth], 52, 54.

Mann, John, 50.
Mansfield, George, 22.
Manwell, Annie (Atwill), vi.
Marchens, Jesse, 54.
Maria, 55.
Mars, 54, 55.
Martial, Saul, 54.
Martin, Daniel, 54.
Martin, John, 54.
• *Mary (transport?)*, 53.
Medoza, Charles, 54.
Menter, Charles, 54.
Merchant, 54.
Mercury, 55.
Mermaid, 54.
Merry, John, 54.
Mesler, Richard, 54.
Miller, Edward, 54.
Miller, John, vi, 3.
Miller, Joseph, 29.
Millet, John, 17.
Millet, Joseph, 14, 19, 22.
Mitchel, Francis, 51.
Mitchel, John, 54.
Monkey (schooner), 1, 11.
Montgomery, John, 54.
Moor, Henry, 54.
Morrison, William, 54.
Mountcalm, Henry, 51.
Mudge, Joseph, 54.

Napoleon, see *Invincible Napoleon (corvette)*.
Nash, Daniel, 54.
Niel, ——, 16.
Nonsuch (schooner), 4, 54.
North Star, 53.
Norton, Edward, 54.

Ogleby, John, 50.
Orene, J., 18.
Orne, Josiah, 15, 16, 17, 19, 20, 22, 23, 24, 26, 27, 28.

Palmer, John, 54.
Parker, William, 54.
Paroga, Joseph, 54.
Paul, ——, 24.
Paul Jones (schooner), 52, 53, 54, 55.
Peacock (sloop), 43.
Penn, William, 50.
Penny, Pain, 51.
Perkins, E., 14.

Perkins, James, 54.
Peters, Aaron, 54.
Peterson, Samuel, 54.
Phillips, Stephen, 50.
Phippen, Israel, 14, 15, 17, 21, 24, 25, 26, 27.
Phippen, John, 14, 15, 16, 17, 20, 22, 23.
Phippen, William, 31.
Pickman, J., 28.
Pierce, Samuel, 54.
Piker, 52.
Pinder, Peter Washington, 14, 16, 18, 19, 20, 22, 23, 24, 25, 26.
Pinkham, Ephra, 54.
Pitman, Joseph, 14, 15, 16, 17, 18, 19, 21, 22, 24, 25.
Place (*brig*), 5.
Pollard, George, 54.
Porter, Charles, 54.
Porter, David, see David Porter.
Porter, Edward A., 15, 18, 20, 23, 25, 26, 28, 64, 65.
Portershan [?], 53.
Potters, G. I., 54.
Potters, John, 54.
President (*frigate*), 22, 52, 53, 54.
Price, ——, 21.
Putnam, see General Putnam.

Rambler, 53.
Rattlesnake (*brig*), 53, 54.
Reed, David, 54.
Reindeer, 43.
Renew, Benjamin, 54.
Rice, Thomas, 55.
Richardson, William, 15.
Ring Dove (*sloop*), vi.
Robberts, John, 50.
Robertson, ——, 17, 24.
Robertson, Frank, 55.
Robertson, Samuel, 55.
Rodgers, Luke, 54.
Rolla, 54.

Saul, Frances, 55.
Saunders, William, 55.
Sawyer, Jed, 55.
Scorpion, 52.
Scudding, Sa. [?], 55.
Sew, Jacob, 55.
Shaw, William, 55.
Sheldon, Henry, 55.

Shepherd, [Sheppard, Shepperd], Samuel, 15, 16, 18, 23, 25, 26.
Shortland, Thomas George, 19, 21, 2, 60, 61.
Shute, William, 18.
Signet (*brig*), 5.
Silsby, Nathaniel, 15.
Simerma, 52.
Simmon, Eben^r, 55.
Simpson, Isaac, 55.
Sinamon, Dan, 55.
Sir Frances Freeland (*packet*), 8.
Siro (*schooner*), 55.
Smart, William, 55.
Smith, Nichol, 55.
Smith, Thomas, 50.
Snap Dragon (*schooner*), 53, 54.
Snow, James, 15, 16, 18, 19, 21.
Steel [?], John, 55.
Story, William, 25.
Stow, John, 55.
Stow, Lewis, 55.
Strout, ——, 16.
Strout, John, 55.
Strout, Joshua, 18.
Studdy, Richard, 55.
Sturtevant, Thomas, *Jr.*, 37, 39.
Sutton, Martin, 55.
Swaysey, ——, 20.
Syren (*brig*), 23, 53, 54.

Tailor, J. B., 55.
Taylor, John, *Sr.*, 16, 35.
Taylor, John, *Jr.*, 16, 35.
Terry, William, 55.
Thomas, Henry, 55.
Thomas, Uriah, 55.
Tickler, 55.
Timmon, M., 55.
Tobby, Elijah, 55.
Tom (*schooner*), 53, 55.
Tomas, John, 55.
Tomkins, K., 55.
Tophouse, Sam, 55.
Trumbull, James, 50.
Turk, see Grand Turk.
Tuttle, Francis, 55.

Upton, Henry, 15, 16, 22, 27.

Valpey, Edna Gertrude, vii.
Valpey, Fred, vi.

pey, George, 11, 31.
pey, Jennie, vi.
pey, Joseph, *Jr.*, v, vi, 29, 64.
pey, Joseph, *Sr.*, v, vi.
pey, Joseph Hodges, v.
pey, Lewis Nelson, v.
pey, Mehitable (Murray), v.
pey, Samuel, 11, 30.
ighn, K., 55.
y, Daniel, 14, 16, 19, 31, 55.
tory (schooner), 52.
er, 55.
gis, James, 55.
id, ——, prize master of, 21.
unteer, 55.

shington, George, birthday celebrated, 22.
shington, John, 50, 60.
sp (sloop), 43, 48.

Wert, George, 55.
Whithan, John, 55.
Whittlebank, Edward, 50.
Wigging, ——, 15.
Wiggins, Richard, 14, 17.
Willet, Robert, 50.
William, 53, 55.
Williams, James, 55.
Williams, James, *of Gayhead*, 55.
Williams, John, 1, 2, 3, 29, 30.
Williams, Thomas, 55.
Willis, B., 1, 3, 29.
Willis, James, 51.
Wilson, Peter, 50.

Yankey, 54, 55.
Young, William, 21, 22, 55.

Zephyr, 53.

Printed in the United Kingdom
by Lightning Source UK Ltd.
131341UK00001B/32/A